SECURITY SURVEILLANCE CENTERS

DESIGN, IMPLEMENTATION, AND OPERATION

SECURITY SURVEILLANCE CENTERS

CENTERS

DESIGN, IMPLEMENTATION, AND OPERATION

Anthony V. DiSalvatore CPP, PSP, PCI, CFE, CLSD

CRC Press
Taylor & Francis Group
Boca Raton London New York

CRC Press is an imprint of the
Taylor & Francis Group, an **informa** business

CRC Press
Taylor & Francis Group
6000 Broken Sound Parkway NW, Suite 300
Boca Raton, FL 33487-2742

First issued in paperback 2019

© 2017 by Taylor & Francis Group, LLC
CRC Press is an imprint of Taylor & Francis Group, an Informa business

No claim to original U.S. Government works

ISBN-13: 978-1-4987-6555-8 (hbk)
ISBN-13: 978-0-367-87794-1 (pbk)

Library of Congress Cataloging-in-Publication Data

Names: DiSalvatore, Anthony V., author.
Title: Security surveillance centers : design, implementation, and operation
/ Anthony V. DiSalvatore.
Description: Boca Raton, FL : CRC Press, [2017]
Identifiers: LCCN 2016047888 | ISBN 9781498765558 (hardback)
Subjects: LCSH: Video surveillance. | Security systems. | Electronic security
systems. | Buildings--Security measures.
Classification: LCC TK6680.3 .D57 2017 | DDC 658.4/73--dc23
LC record available at https://lccn.loc.gov/2016047888

Visit the Taylor & Francis Web site at
http://www.taylorandfrancis.com

and the CRC Press Web site at
http://www.crcpress.com

Dedication

This book is dedicated to my son Remo and my daughter Andriana, who teach me something new about myself every day and are the driving force behind my desire to make the world a better place. As you have entered adulthood, I am amazed at your sense of ownership of any situation, and how you base your decisions on how they will positively impact those around you. You both have chosen to take the road less traveled, have embraced the mantra of being true to yourself, and inspire me, on a daily basis, by your thoughts and actions.

I could not possibly be more proud of both of you and the courage, tenacity, and wisdom you have displayed as you embark on your journey into the world. This is only the beginning of your adventure, and I have no doubt that you will achieve great things on every level in life as you pursue your dreams and capture your passions.

Love you
Proud of you
Respect you
I am with you always

Love,
DAD

Contents

Preface

Ever since I can remember, I have always wanted to protect others. One of my earliest recollections was when I was in the fourth grade when I was waiting for the morning bell to ring for class at my elementary school. I noticed a second grader crying, and I walked over and asked him what was wrong. He pointed to a sixth grader who was standing next to him, who to me seemed like he was 6 feet tall. The crying boy sobbed that he took his ball. I asked this giant of a boy to give the ball back. He shook his head and refused, saying, "No, what are you going to do about it?" I don't know what came over me, but I curled my hand up in a fist and punched him in the jaw. The ball fell out of his hand, bounced once, and I grabbed it and handed it to the crying boy, who smiled as he looked at the ball in his hand.

The sixth grader was seething with anger, and I took off. The sixth grader then picked up a rock and hurled it at me, striking me in the head, directly behind my left ear. I fell to the ground, placed my hand over the wound, and then stood up quickly and began running again. The sixth grader gave chase as I ran toward the school and I noticed he stopped chasing me as I was nearing the school doors. I felt a warm liquid pouring through my hand and suddenly noticed blood was falling to the ground.

I entered the school doors and started running to the nurse's office. My fourth grade teacher, Mr. Schuda, shouted, "Walk." I started walking and removed my hand from my head and blood began to go all over the floor. Mr. Schuda then shouted, "Run." I ran to the nurse's office where she called my mom and wrapped bandages around my head. When my mom arrived to the nurse's office, she took me to the emergency room. The doctor gave me 12 stitches and explained that he could not really close the wound because a piece of the meat behind my ear was gone—somewhere on the playground was a piece of my head. I never heard of it ever being found—an animal must have eaten it. When I returned back to school the next day, the school imposed a new rule—no rock throwing. I never did find out if Wilson Bull, the kid who hit me with the rock, was ever suspended or anything. That was the first time I met him, and I never saw him again. There are many more tales to tell about adventures that I have been involved in over the years where I have sustained injury while trying to protect others—but that is for perhaps another book and another time.

I feel I was born with an innate passion to protect others with a disregard for my own well-being, as I am sure that many in security and law enforcement–related fields have felt. As I am entering the twilight of my career pursuing these endeavors, I wanted to put together a book that would be useful to those who have the tremendous responsibility of keeping others safe and protecting assets with the aid of a security surveillance center. The other passion that I have is mentoring others who are entering this arena and helping provide guidance and direction to them as they pursue their careers. With these things in mind, I have asked myself constantly while writing this book, "What would I have found useful, when establishing myself in this field?" My hope is that this book is many things to many people on a lot of different levels.

The term *security surveillance center* is a hybrid of two areas, that early in my career were distinctly different and were not frequently intertwined. As the decades have passed, and businesses have stressed and emphasized the importance of working smarter not harder, it was only a matter of time before these two areas were joined together. In the end, the return on investment and the synergy a security surveillance center creates make good business sense, to form, establish, and operate one, if one is not already in place.

To the point of this book being many things to many people, the information on the following pages can be used by any business, regardless of its shape or size. This book is helpful to any business that has a CCTV system. Whether the business has a handful of employees or thousands of employees, there is a lot of information for the reader to use. The basics pertaining to the law, procedure, and operation remain relatively the same regardless of the size of the operation. However, in your particular jurisdiction, it is important to keep abreast of the laws, best practices, and developments in this area for the protection of everyone on both sides of the cameras.

I have spent a lifetime wanting to protect others. With the ever-changing world events and the increase of violence and terrorist attacks on the rise in the world arena, it is now more important than ever for companies, businesses, and corporations to safely protect their guests, employees, and assets from those who wish to disrupt their daily operations, cause harm to others, or create an umbrella of fear. One important layer and aspect of providing this protection is the development and operation of a security surveillance center. The security surveillance center is the nerve center of any security or protective operation. Cameras are monitored and reviewed on a consistent basis to detect any situations that appear unusual or out of the ordinary. In the event that something is detected that does not look right, in-house and local authorities are alerted with the pertinent details and respond accordingly. Emergency calls for help, assistance, and general communication to and from employees, guests, and operatives in the field all use security surveillance centers as their conduit.

The proper training of personnel and utilizing the proper tools and equipment in this area are critical for the safety and security of all. This enables quick and accurate responses to alarms, dispatching personnel to the proper locations, and calmly and professionally gathering information from emergency calls and alarms. Personnel consistently demonstrating the ability to execute the key components of the security surveillance center's operation are a sure sign that they have been trained properly and have a solid understanding of their roles and responsibilities.

This book goes into detail on these topics and many more crucial areas that can improve the effectiveness and efficiency of any operation. It is designed to be a great resource for existing operation centers or can be used to create a security surveillance center, if one does not exist, explaining the steps involved in creating one.

Over the past few years, the pricing of CCTV equipment has made it affordable for every type of business and organization. At first glance, this seems like a great benefit. However, without the proper protocol, procedures, and training in place, the results could be disastrous by exposing the operators to civil and possibly criminal consequences.

This user-friendly book addresses concerns of a wide range of users, from national organizations to mom-and-pop operations and can be applied to any organization that has CCTV systems in place. On one hand, this book is a great asset for organizations of any size that are setting up CCTV systems by providing insight and examples of forms, policies, design, best practices, and so on. On the other hand, this book is a great training guide for those who supervise and operate a security surveillance center. A test question and answer section in Chapter 9 allows the owner of a business or manager of a department to test the knowledge of security surveillance center personnel to ensure that the information contained in this book has been absorbed and the personnel of the security surveillance center are functioning within the standards of the industry and the boundaries of the law.

This book examines the critical areas of design, implementation, and operation of security surveillance centers regardless of their size. Areas that will be discussed and explained in detail include the role of a security surveillance center, overview of the control room and console design, processes, procedures, legal perspectives, forms, professionalism, glossary of terms and definitions, and question and answer sections. Unlike other books on the market that pertain to surveillance that are very technology-driven, this book focuses on the operation of a security surveillance center. This book is applicable to audiences ranging from anyone who has a small, relatively simple system to industry giants who have facilities across the country. Among other things, this book is meant to be a training/testing tool for leaders/operators and a guide for establishing standard operating procedures (SOPs), policies, protocols, and forms to be used for the operation of a security surveillance center.

Unique components of this book include detailed forms that may be utilized in the operation of a security surveillance center. This book delves into areas where documentation of events and situations are critical in safeguarding the operations and assets of the organization. One example of the many forms contained in this publication is the chain of custody forms. These are used to demonstrate chain of custody when issuing security surveillance coverage to law enforcement or outside agencies. Other types of forms that are located in the back matter section simply titled, "Forms," are the forms used in the day-to-day operation that demonstrate that the security surveillance center is performing their due diligence. There are also step-by-step processes and procedures located in Chapters 3 and 4, titled, "Security Surveillance Center Processes" and "Security Surveillance Center Procedures," respectively. These chapters provide you with examples on how these critical items can be worded and constructed.

Legal perspectives, the Fourth Amendment, and the importance of professionalism are discussed in Chapter 6 and the impact of the critical role of each is explained. Examples of practices that have performed well in these areas are reviewed, and those that have not are examined. The tremendous downside of operating in the gray area or not following legal trends is explored along with the upside of staying abreast of legal developments and the Fourth Amendment. For example, in the opinion of many scholars, when video surveillance of public areas is continuous, it generally does not present significant legalities. Legal interpretations of the Fourth Amendment as it pertains to video surveillance appear to be in favor of CCTV systems use to protect the public. The belief is that continuous video surveillance does not intrude upon an individual's sphere of privacy; it simply records events occurring in public space for which individuals do not have reasonable expectations of privacy. This as well as the importance of personnel understanding the significant difference between foreseeability and the totality of circumstances approaches and the role each plays in court decisions are also examined.

This book contains personal insight and situations that I have been directly involved with, worked closely with others on, or researched. For example, "just doesn't look right" (Chapter 7, JDLR) is an area that is discussed as it pertains to one of the most valuable tools that security surveillance center personnel have—or can develop. The power of observation of the actions taken by others and recognizing when something JDLR and being able to put the pieces of the puzzle together is an invaluable tool and critical for a security surveillance center to be successful. It also helps to quantify the performance and value of the security surveillance center and its operators by documenting the prevention of incidents, providing tangible cases, and documenting actual incidents.

The following is a personal story of JDLR in action that occurred in my rookie year as a law enforcement officer. Late at night, my lieutenant and I were on patrol when I observed a white male carrying a plastic milk crate with some items in it. My instincts told me that this just doesn't look right, and I advised my lieutenant of the observation. The patrol vehicle was turned around, and when the subject who was walking with the milk crate saw the patrol vehicle, he immediately placed the crate on the ground. The subject advised that he had found the items contained in the milk crate—stereo equipment—in a dumpster and was taking it home. At that moment, a report came in that a nearby home was burglarized and—you guessed it—stereo equipment was stolen. With proper training, this "instinct" can be developed in security surveillance centers and can aid in the well-being of the guest, company, and assets.

A glossary of terms and definitions is located at the back of the book and Chapter 9 contains test questions and answers. This metric measurement will enable you to determine if the material and contents of this book have been absorbed and retained, or if there are areas that need additional review. This component will assist leaders of security surveillance centers to ascertain if their operators have the necessary knowledge needed to be effective and efficient in the operation of a security surveillance center.

The following is a brief synopsis of each chapter:

Chapter 1: Building Stages and the Critical Role of Security Surveillance Centers
This chapter explores the steps involved in building a security surveillance center. The steps are reviewed and discussed, including planning, design, requests for proposals, vendor selection, lessons learned, equipment, alarms, key control, and heightened alert procedures.

Also, the role of today's operator in the modern security surveillance center is similar to that of a conductor of an orchestra. Security surveillance center personnel are the maestro of the operation of the security surveillance team as it relates to the tempo of which personnel are dispatched to incidents.

Chapter 2: Overview of the Control Room and Console Design
The proper design of the security surveillance center console room is discussed and examined. This area is one of the most critical components of any security surveillance center program. The security surveillance center's location, layout, and console design are some of the most important factors in determining the overall success and operation of the security surveillance center.

Chapter 3: Security Surveillance Center Processes
Security surveillance center processes and best practices are examined, and how they are designed to provide maximum protection, identification, and detection of any activity or crisis that could impact the property are explained. Implementation of these processes and best practices will enable the security surveillance center to provide a safe, secure environment and produce usable video to determine the sequence of events of an incident and the visual facts as they relate to a situation.

Chapter 4: Security Surveillance Center Procedures
Various methods of developing and implementing security surveillance procedures will be reviewed. Strict adherence to policy and procedures is the foundation on which a successful security surveillance center relies upon to be effective and efficient. Procedures are living documents and should be reviewed and updated every 6 to 12 months. When revisions are made, it is important to put in the date of revision on the procedure and to keep the old copy of the procedure that was revised. This is useful for legal and performance issues to determine what procedure was in effect at the time that an incident occurred. The life, safety, and security of an organization and the internal and external guests depend on the knowledge that is exhibited by security surveillance center personnel. It is important that security surveillance center personnel demonstrate that the information contained in the standard operating procedures has been absorbed and retained. One way to measure this is how the performance of security surveillance center personnel meshes with the standard operating procedures.

Chapter 5: Fire Command
An intricate part of a security surveillance center is the fire command center (FCC). The importance of the location, processes, procedures, and protocol are examined and reviewed.

Chapter 6: Legal Perspectives, Ethics, and the Fourth Amendment
Professionals generally exhibit behavior that is focused, accountable, confident, competent, goal oriented, respectful, and has a sense of urgency. Security surveillance center professionals do not react emotionally when handling stressful situations. Critical situations are handled in a serious, effective, and efficient manner. Some of the major elements of professionalism are a code of ethics, philosophy, knowledge, guidelines, and standardization of job performance. The code of ethics plays a key role in developing synergy and integrating the other key components that help establish professionalism in a security surveillance center.

In the opinion of many scholars, when video surveillance of public areas is continuous, it generally does not present significant legalities. Interpretations of the Fourth Amendment as it pertains to video surveillance appear to be in favor of the use of CCTV to protect the public. The belief is that continuous video surveillance does not intrude upon an individual's sphere of privacy; it simply records events occurring in public space for which individuals do not have reasonable expectations of privacy.

It is important that security surveillance personnel understand the significant difference between foreseeability and totality of the circumstances approaches and the role each plays in court decisions.

Chapter 7: Audits, Thefts, and Effective Patrol Methods
This chapter reviews various effective techniques and methods that should be utilized in the detection of violations, theft, and embezzlement. One of the most valuable tools of security surveillance center personnel is the power of observation and the ability to piece that together with actions taken by those under observation to recognize when something JDLR.

Chapter 8: Training
The selection and training of the security surveillance center personnel are among the most important aspects of this area. Being a member of the security surveillance center should be a coveted position of which, in the proper environment, one should not merely apply for a job, but be invited to join the team. It is important to invest time and money into the training of security surveillance center personnel for many reasons, including the safety of guests, visitors, and employees. A well-selected and trained security surveillance center team will ultimately help to improve profit margins by identifying and detecting suspicious activity and those committing these acts.

Chapter 9: Test Questions
This chapter covers components discussed throughout the book. This is a metric measurement that can be used to determine if the reader has absorbed contents or if there are areas that need additional review.

Glossary
Terms and definitions related to security surveillance centers.

Forms
Various forms utilized by the security surveillance center are contained in this section. These forms are a valuable resource and serve as an excellent guide for tracking operational functions and responsibilities, documenting information, aiding in the efficient, organized, accurate, and professional operation of the security surveillance center.

Acknowledgments

It has been an honor and a privilege to have the opportunity to publish a book in an area that I feel is very important in this day and age. I am grateful to have had the opportunity to be involved in security-related positions for more than 30 years and to have worked shoulder to shoulder with so many fine men and women. I have been truly blessed and am grateful to have been gifted with a passion for helping others and with a mindset of making a positive difference in this world, while using security-related fields as my conduit.

I would like to thank my family and friends who have helped and guided me throughout my life, and continue to do so. Although over the years, miles have come between us, they are always in my thoughts and prayers and continue to provide support to me both emotionally and spiritually. I have learned vicariously through them by both their actions and good intentions.

This support has helped guide me and brought me to my focus on helping and mentoring others. At this stage of my life and career, I am thankful to be in a position where I am able to mentor young people who are entering into the realm of the security surveillance profession. Amazingly, my passion grows stronger every day, and I hope that you are fortunate enough to have found your niche in life and are able to achieve success while helping others.

Author

Anthony V. DiSalvatore, CPP, PSP, PCI, CFE, CLSD, has over 30 years of experience in security-related positions. He has been involved in the opening of numerous casinos, hotels, and entertainment complexes, ranging in value from hundreds of millions of dollars to billions of dollars. Anthony has been involved from the ground up on the design, implementation, and operation of security surveillance centers at various properties across the country. He served as a state trooper for the New Jersey State Police and received a Distinguished Service Award for actions taken—the highest honor that is bestowed upon a trooper.

Anthony has also been recognized for actions taken while working at large properties in South Florida, New Jersey, and New York City. He performed an integral role during Hurricanes Frances and Wilma in South Florida, Hurricane Sandy in New Jersey, and the largest power outage in US history in New York City by ensuring that business continuity and disaster recovery plans were executed.

Anthony earned an associate degree in arts and science from Gloucester County College, Sewell, New Jersey; a bachelor's degree in law justice from Glassboro State College, Glassboro, New Jersey; and master's degrees in education administration from Seton Hall University, South Orange, New Jersey, and criminal justice from Rutgers University, Newark, New Jersey. Anthony is a member of the American Society for Industrial Security (ASIS) International and the Gaming and Wagering Protection Council; has previously held membership in the Crime and Loss Prevention Council, and Business Management and Business Continuity Council; and has been recognized by ASIS as a Triple Crown recipient by being a Certified Protection Professional (CPP), Physical Security Professional (PSP), and Professional Certified Investigator (PCI).

Anthony is also a Certified Fraud Examiner and Certified Lodging Security Director and has presented at numerous venues across the country. He has also been treasurer of the Las Vegas Security Chiefs Association and the gaming subsector lead in the Department of Homeland Security Commercial Facilities Coordinating Council and possesses a Secret Level Clearance.

At this stage in life, Anthony enjoys mentoring and educating those entering the security and surveillance realm. He finds it rewarding to mold and guide the next generation toward their potential and provide guidance toward their career path. Anthony finds it very rewarding to teach others to believe in themselves, their abilities, to always do the right thing, and make good life choices.

The following is one recent example of a letter received from a mentee, "I just received a new role in my job and it requires a lot of my time now. I want to thank you for believing in me and giving me a chance to prove to my peers and myself that I could succeed if I worked hard enough—Thank you." Anthony believes that having an impact on others in a positive way and playing a part in making better lives for others is more important than any degree or title and makes him the richest man in the world.

1 Building Stages and the Critical Role of Security Surveillance Centers

The following is a result of my many years dedicated to developing and establishing security surveillance centers in various industries. Security surveillance centers are sometimes referred to as monitor rooms, dispatch centers, surveillance rooms, and so on. In areas that have historically kept security and surveillance separated, there appears to be a paradigm shift developing in the field driven by the economy, safety concerns, protection of others, and the synergistic effect that occurs when these two critical areas are combined.

When security and surveillance are combined to create a security surveillance center, it creates a more efficient and effective operation that functions as a cohesive team. This acts as a force multiplier for any operation by creating an instantaneous flow of information, the immediate response to situations, and the calibration of thinking on how security and surveillance concerns are addressed. For those companies, businesses, and industries that do not operate in this manner, the hope is that after being exposed to the information in this book a *eureka* moment will occur, and the next logical evolution for those who have security and surveillance areas separate will be to combine them into one.

Expanding the role of the security surveillance professional is a positive approach in combating a tough economy and can help recession-proof and solidify the role of a security surveillance center in progressive-thinking organizations. Conversely, when this approach is not implemented and the leadership teams in organizations feel great pressure to improve the bottom line, a decision may be made to randomly reduce security and surveillance staffing levels. Being penny-wise and pound-foolish places the security, surveillance, and safety of all involved on the precipice of a very slippery slope. It is a gamble that does not have a long-term payoff and is indicative of an organization that may be taking desperate measures to survive. The negative impacts of litigation and the courts awarding in favor of the plaintiff could take years to recover from or could be the final event that puts a company out of business.

Hopefully, this book will shed some light on areas that were unknown prior to the reading of this book or will help to clarify questions or concerns pertaining to establishing security surveillance centers. In crafting this book, it was my desire that readers will be able to increase their knowledge in areas that were unfamiliar and use this book as a reference guide for training and establishing a new security surveillance center standard in the industry.

Throughout my career, I have been involved in the design, installation, and operation of security surveillance centers at various venues across the country.

1

There are several ways in which a security surveillance center comes into existence: construction of a new property or project, addition to or expansion of an existing security surveillance center, or the building of one from scratch. In some instances, the leadership in organizations or projects needed to be convinced of the benefits and the need of a security surveillance center prior to granting approval for the project.

In these cases to increase the chances of having the security surveillance center project approved, the following should be outlined, explained, and discussed with leadership: return on investment (ROI), deterrents, displacement, system design, installation, and operation. In properties where security and surveillance operate separately, they can be combined to streamline cost, increase productivity, and enhance communications. Combining security and surveillance departments into one department saves money and combines areas of responsibility with the benefits of reducing manpower and reducing budgets, while increasing performance and operating in an effective and efficient manner.

The ROI of the implementation of a security surveillance center should be clearly explained to leadership. The ROI is used to explain the benefit and profit to a facility—it answers the question: "what are they getting for their money?" This explanation should include the approximate number of additional investigative cases, policy violations, or safety issues that will be discovered by the use of the implementation or expansion of a security surveillance center. For example, advise leadership of approximately how many employee theft cases you anticipate generating by adding a security surveillance center operator. If the number of theft cases generated is forecasted to recover money, property, or restitution equal to or greater than the salary for the added position, then it will have a good chance of being approved. However, be careful not to exaggerate or embellish the anticipated results, because you may be held accountable for your forecast in the upcoming budget year.

The deterrent effect that a proactive security surveillance center will have on employees and wrongdoers should be explained to leadership. In order for a deterrent to be effective, it must be swift, certain, and severe. If one of these components is missing, the deterrent effect will not have as great of an impact. In the operation of a proactive security surveillance center, theft or policy violations will be observed and recorded and the violator will be detected, interviewed, and issued appropriate disciplinary action by the department of human resources. When employees and wrongdoers become aware that when offenses or violations occur they will be addressed in a swift, certain, and severe manner, it will deter them from committing these acts.

The displacement effect that a proactive security surveillance center will have for a facility should be explained to leadership. With the addition or expansion of a security surveillance center, including overt cameras, signage indicating that closed-circuit television (CCTV) is in use displayed on the perimeter, parking lots, stores, and so on, wrongdoers will be passively advised not to commit undesirable acts on the premises. Instead those with criminal intent will not take a chance of committing crime that may be captured on CCTV at the facility. They will relocate, or displace, their criminal behavior to another location away from the premises and facility. The goal of the implementation of a security surveillance center in terms of the displacement effect is not to prevent criminal activity, although it would be nice if we could, but to not have criminal activity occur on our property or facility.

In order to justify the installation or improvements of a security surveillance center to the leaders of an organization, the following items must be reviewed and taken into consideration so that a realistic budget can be developed.

- *Design*: The drawings, blueprints, type of system, and components are determined in this phase. This would include monitors, servers, computers, intrusion detection devices, sensors, detectors, card readers, cameras, conduits, wiring, and consultants.
- *Installation*: This is one of the most expensive items of the project. This includes permits and the costs and installation of various sensors, contacts, and access control devices to the security surveillance center system. Once the system is installed, there will be ongoing operational costs associated with the operation of the system.
- *Operation*: The operation of the system includes staffing, training, policy, and procedures.
- *Information technology–related expenses*: These costs include anti-virus technology, system patches, backup and archiving, and database management.
- *Maintenance*: These expenses include upgrades to the software, emergency repairs, keeping the domes on the cameras clean, and keeping the system in good working order.
- *Replacement*: Prior to the purchase of the system for the security surveillance center, the life cycle of the system should be determined and the approximate replacement cost should be calculated. Usually, the best way to present this information is to assign a cost and anticipate the life range for each item.

The system design, installation, and operation should be reviewed with the leadership team so that they can make an informed decision regarding the security surveillance center. This would include the addition or upgrading of sensors, detectors, contacts, access control, equipment, and staffing. The cost and need of various types and placement of sensors, detectors, and card readers, including fire, heat, smoke, water flow, motion, and passive infrared sensor detection devices should be examined and discussed. The recommendation is that all sensors, detectors, and devices should report to the security surveillance center.

One of the more costly areas of implementing or upgrading a security surveillance center is the installation of the system. The areas covered under the cost of the installation include the servers, computers, monitors, and control panel. Since security surveillance centers are computer based, the IT department has a significant role in the installation, operation, and ongoing growth and protection of the security surveillance center systems. It is important that property leadership understands the role and importance of the IT department when it comes to the proper operation of the technical aspects of a security surveillance center and does not attempt to have security surveillance center operators be responsible for this critical area. Sometimes this occurs when property leadership does not fully understand the complexity of this area, and in an effort to keep expenses down to meet budgetary demands, has non-IT personnel oversee this highly volatile area who do not have the proper skill set or knowledge. This is the job and responsibility of the leader of the security surveillance center to effectively communicate the importance and complexity of this area to the decision-makers of the leadership team of the property and make a persuading argument to have skilled, trained, and responsible IT personnel oversee this critical area.

Regardless of the size of the security surveillance center, the following general guidelines should be implemented to ensure the successful completion and maintenance of the project. Planning of the requirements and objectives of the security surveillance center is one of the first steps that should be undertaken. For example, layers of protection should be installed to safeguard the operators and equipment of the security surveillance center. The many layers available should be discussed with leadership. Sabotage, protection from intruders, and intentional harm caused by internal employees are some of the topics that should be discussed with leadership regarding the securing and protection of the security surveillance center.

Leadership should be made aware that although no one particular process or method is ever 100% effective in the protection of any asset, the best approach is to implement layers of protection that become increasingly difficult to defeat in close proximity to an asset. In the circumstance of the protection of the security surveillance center, the methods and processes of protection should be reviewed and discussed with leadership and should include the following:

- Only authorized personnel should be permitted in the security surveillance center. Those who do not have a "need to know" should not be granted access.
- The security surveillance center should have signage on the entry door indicating that only authorized personnel are permitted. There should also be signage indicating that food and drink are prohibited.
- The security surveillance center should have a combination of authentication methods at the entrance to the room such as a badge reader, biometric reader, internal door controls, pin code, and so forth.
- A discussion of the types and value of internal door controls to increase control of the entry and exit of the security surveillance center should be explained with leadership. For example, a mantrap will only allow the door leading into the security surveillance center to open after the outer door is closed. For additional security, the mantrap can be combined with other devices such as a card reader, biometrics, or a door release controlled by personnel located within the security surveillance center. This type of protective system can be very expensive and should only be implemented if deemed necessary by the leadership team.
- The security surveillance center should have redundant methods of communication, including two-way radio, telephone, cell phone, and so on.
- No one should have access to the security surveillance center without being accompanied by security surveillance center personnel. At no time should a member of the cleaning crew, facilities, and so on, ever be left alone without an escort.

- Before any escort into the security surveillance center is permitted, all sensitive items must be placed out of sight or placed in a nonviewable mode. This includes photos, reports, monitors, and so on.
- Role, function, and location of the security surveillance center should be carefully considered. To protect against flood damage to the CCTV equipment and other electronics, the security surveillance center should never be placed in the basement or below sea level.
- Review and discuss the need for backup power to the security surveillance center (i.e., backup generators and/or battery power).

Once all of the planning and objectives of the security surveillance center are established, the next step is to schedule a meeting to review and discuss the design, scope, and budget with the leaders of the project and property. The contact information of the key players should be exchanged and a meeting schedule should be established, usually once a week, to review the progress of the project and any pitfalls or concerns that need to be addressed. During these meetings, after it is determined exactly what equipment is needed, where all the cameras are to be installed, the functions the system is to perform, and where and how the security surveillance center will be located and operated, the next step is to select a vendor.

Questions to consider when designing the security surveillance center are exactly what are the needs, what are the expectations from leadership, and exactly what will the personnel in this area be performing. It is important that there be communication between leadership, the project leader, and the person ultimately responsible for the operation of the security surveillance center. For example, some questions that need to be addressed during the design phase includes the following: Will keys be distributed to employees from this area? Will employee and vendor badges be produced and distributed from this area? Will door alarms report to the security surveillance center? Will the operators be responsible for identifying and allowing access to sensitive areas via CCTV, card swipe, and badge? Once identified, will operator access be granted by pressing a button or clicking on an icon on the computer? Will the fire command center be located in this area, and if so, will the operators be responsible for monitoring the panel, dispatching personnel, contacting the fire department, and making announcements over the public address system? If any of the above are going to be in the area of responsibility of the security surveillance center, then this must be vetted, communicated, and understood by all involved, and this will have an impact on the scope of the design.

A lot of thought has to go into every aspect of the design. For example, something that seems like a simple decision regarding the window that will be installed in the security surveillance center at first appears to be an easy one. However, after closer examination, it is more complex than one would think. How large should the window be? Will the window be tinted? Will the window be one-way glass? Will it slide open and closed or will it have an opening cut into it where keys, badges, and other items can be distributed? The window location that will be used by the operators will have to be placed in an area that does not permit employees to view any of the camera views, alarms, and so on.

Once these areas are thoroughly vetted and discussed with the decision-makers and leaders of the property, research and selection of systems or products should be conducted. This includes the specifications of equipment, software, and hardware. The manufacturer of the systems or products selected should be contacted and asked questions regarding the system or product, including:

- Life cycle of the system or product
- Maintenance cycle of system or product
- When potential changes or upgrades are expected to occur
- Life expectancy of system or product

There is a direct correlation of the extent of responsibilities and functions that the operators of a security surveillance center perform with the number of personnel needed to monitor and operate the various areas including CCTV, alarms, phones, badge making, distribution of badges, keys, and so on. There are many areas that must be addressed and resolved prior to the selection of a vendor and the construction or modification of a security surveillance center that many times go undetected by the inexperienced or leaders who are new to the security surveillance center world. For this reason, it is very important for those with the experience and knowledge to thoroughly explain the options available and the requirements needed to operate effectively and efficiently. When this communication does not occur, or the leadership lacks the experience or knowledge in this area, unrealistic time lines may be set on the completion, operation, and training of the personnel in a security surveillance center. This usually results in a rush to get things done, equipment that is not operational or performing at its full potential, and items having to be installed or addressed later.

Only after all questions regarding specific equipment, design, operation, responsibilities, and functions of the security surveillance center have been addressed and answered should the project move on to the next step of the construction phase. If vendors have not been selected, a search should be conducted to prequalify vendors before sending them a request for proposal (RFP) or invitation for bid (IFB) on the project. In effect, the vendor is an extension of the company and should require the same amount of effort and due dligence as hiring a new employee. If possible, it is usually best to identify at least three qualified vendors for the project. If circumstances permit the completion of this process, it will save time when sending out the RFP or IFB. Instead of sending it out to all available vendors, it can be sent out to only those who have been prequalified.

It is important for the person spearheading the construction of the security surveillance center (usually the leader of the security or loss prevention team) to do his or her due diligence when narrowing the search for the best-suited vendor to complete the project. The vendor should have at least three references that are closely related to the construction of security surveillance centers, and they should have adequate general liability insurance. This amount will be determined by the size and scope of the project and property—usually between $1 million and $2 million of general liability insurance.

About a week or two after the RFP is issued, a comprehensive walk-through and meeting should be scheduled where the project is to be completed. This allows the vendors to see the exact location where the security surveillance center will be installed.

This also shows the vendors who wish to bid on the project that they have competition, which could result in the vendors submitting bids that come in, at, or below budget. Immediately after the walk-through, all vendors and the person spearheading the project should meet in a conference room. Prior to the start of the meeting, the project leader should place a audio recorder in the middle of the table, and after the leader has everyone's attention, he or she should begin the meeting by turning on the audio recorder stating name, title, date, time, location and that this meeting is being audio recorded. Then each vendor should state his or her name, company name, and that he or she realizes that this meeting is being audio recorded. This is helpful for the project leader to accurately recall exactly what was discussed.

During the meeting, the requirements of the project can be discussed as well as the minimum level of insurance the vendors must have in order to bid on the project. If the project involves linking systems and equipment to an existing security surveillance center, plans regarding the retrofit of these areas should be reviewed. These plans should include any new buildings or rooms that are being added and identification of camera locations and access control systems. The following illustrates an add-on to a project pertaining to access control measures regarding entry into security surveillance center areas.

If an existing security surveillance center system is being upgraded or replaced, the area where the CCTV cameras are viewed should be visited. The specific location where the new equipment is to be installed should be identified and discussed. Every location where a digital video recorder (DVR) or network video recorder (NVR) is located should be physically visited, the total number of each should be documented, and it should be documented if the DVR or NVR is currently on the network. The following is an example of how each should be documented:

- *Location 1*: Two 16-channel DVR (analog)
  - Fixed 14 DVR 1, 16 DVR 2
  - PTZ 2 DVR 1
  - Not on network

Vendors should ask questions and receive answers that are helpful for them to bid the project accurately. The benefit of having this meeting with all possible vendors in the same room is that it ensures that they all hear the same answers to the questions that are raised. It also is a big time saver for the project leader in that he or she does not have to answer the same question multiple times. If a particular brand, type, or model of equipment is required, it is important to advise the vendor of this and any other specific requirements, such as project start date and expected completion date. Also, in order to avoid confusion on what the definition of "completed" is, the project leader should clearly explain what the expectations are for the project to be considered completed. This is the time when the project leader should discuss if the vendor who is awarded the project is going to be penalized if the security surveillance center is not completed on time, and what that per day penalty is. Generally, the penalty is a specific dollar amount that is deducted from the final payment to the vendor at the completion of the project. The date that all bids are to be received and whom they are to be received by should be reviewed and clarified if necessary. If during the bidding process additional questions arise from the vendors, an additional meeting should be held to answer any additional questions from the vendors. This ensures that all vendors receive the same information and that all vendors are playing on a level field.

Before making a final decision on who is awarded the contract, the vendor should be interviewed and asked about the experience the vendor has on working on projects that are closely related to security surveillance centers. This will help provide insight into the vendor's involvement in other similar projects. The businesses that had projects that the vendor was involved with in the past should be contacted and, among other things, asked if the project was completed on time and if the business would hire the vendor again.

Once a final decision is made, and a vendor has been awarded the contract, the project leader should conduct scheduled regular periodic meetings where progress, challenges, and opportunities are discussed. It is recommended that these meetings be conducted while walking through the site and physically checking the areas with the vendor. This makes it easier to explain and discuss any issues that need to be addressed and ensures that the layout is exactly how it should be.

It is important to ensure that the physical layout of the installation matches the plans and that everyone is working off of the same set of plans. I have been on projects that have involved multiple vendors and each was working off a different set of plans. This occurs when revised plans are not distributed properly and/or do not have the date listed on the plan of the revision. For example, one day a wall would go up, the next day it would be taken down, and the next day the wall would go up again. This leads to a waste of time and money. The best way to resolve this from occurring is to call a meeting with all vendors involved and issue the revised plans. It is important to retrieve the old version of the plans that were issued and distribute the updated time-stamped plans.

Many times during the construction or expansion of a project, the intricate details pertaining to a security surveillance center and all of the areas of responsibility associated with it are overlooked or flat out missed. One reason this occurs is because of overlapping devices reporting to multiple departments, where each department thinks the other department is addressing the need. For this reason, it is important that the leader of the project should not assume that others will address the needs of his or her area and have the mindset that all roads regarding the security surveillance center lead to and through him or her. Other reasons this may occur include lack of knowledge, experience, or attention to detail.

The following are some lessons learned from projects I have been involved with in the past when working with vendors on the installation of security surveillance centers. When pulling cable through conduit, the minimum conduit size should be at least one-half inch. It is best to go with a larger size and pull extra cable through the conduit during the initial installation. The additional expense is minimal and makes the system ready for future expansion. If this is not done during the initial cable pull, it could prevent or delay future expansion plans due to the high costs associated with the labor involved with pulling additional cable. For example, I was working at a property that did not have a CCTV system and my task was to develop a security surveillance center with a very limited budget. The initial prices received were well above our budget for the project. Being frustrated and disappointed that the project may have to wait until the following year, I asked a vendor, whom I had done business with in the past, if the cost could be cut significantly if we pulled the cable with our in-house team and the vendor made all the connections to the system (cameras, DVR, etc.). After several meetings, the vendor agreed to work on the project and allow the property to pull the cable. In this case, pulling the cable was very labor intensive and resulted in the initial cost of the project being cut in half, since we pulled the cable.

Many times, security surveillance centers are viewed by leadership as being non–revenue generating departments. Because of this, it can be difficult to have companies allocate large amounts of money in the budget for projects such as the one previously described. Keep this example in mind if you should find yourself in a similar situation where a project's estimated expense is more than the money allocated for it in the budget.

Another example of a real-life experience that I have been involved with regarding the construction of a new property and a security surveillance center pertains to a vendor being extremely behind schedule. I was contacted by a general manager and asked to meet and speak with the vendor. The reason the leader of the project and department was taken out of the loop was because he would have to keep and continue to develop his relationship with the vendor. After meeting and walking through the project and reviewing the deadlines that were missed, a direct discussion was held between the vendor and I. The outcome was that the vendor agreed to pull the rest of his technicians off of all other projects and work around the clock—even though it was during a holiday season—to meet the deadline. This resulted in the project being completed on schedule, and the leader of the area was able to maintain and develop a great rapport with the vendor. If you should ever find yourself involved in circumstances as the one previously described, it is important to meet with the leader of the area prior to meeting and reviewing the project with the vendor. This will prevent any damage to your relationship with the project leader, and the leader will not be blindsided or learn about your involvement secondhand. Believe me, the project leader will be greatly appreciative of the consideration and honesty exhibited and will strongly support you throughout your career.

It is important to establish good communications with vendors who work on your security surveillance center. On projects that I have been involved in that were new properties, the following method was used to assist in communicating where cameras should be located. During the construction phase of a new property where the floors are concrete, and carpet is installed near the completion of the project. This method helped to ensure that the cameras were placed in the proper areas. I spray-painted a circle with an "X" in the middle of it to represent where pan-tilt-zoom (PTZ) cameras are to be installed. Using the same principle, a rectangle with a triangle on the short side of it, pointing to where the camera view should be pointed, is spray-painted on the floor. The cameras should also be numbered on the plan and on the images spray-painted on the unfinished concrete floor. This makes it easier for everyone involved in the project.

Finally, the day arrives when the security surveillance center is completed and all of the equipment is installed and functioning properly. Thought has to be given to the maintenance of all of the equipment associated with the security surveillance center. I have found that it is best to deal with a single vendor, preferably the vendor who did the initial installation of the project. This prevents what I like to call, "what came first the chicken or the egg situations." Simply put, when a vendor other than the vendor who installed a system is contacted to work on the system, the vendor will have to troubleshoot and start from ground zero. This takes time and costs money. Then, over the course of time, when multiple vendors are used, and multiple repairs or adjustments have been made and the system has reoccurring issues, vendors will sometimes point fingers at the other vendors who have been involved and state that the issue is a result of their work on the project, lack of attention to detail, and so on. This makes it very hard to trace back who did exactly what work on the system and have the previous vendor repair the work previously performed for free—if it is under the warranty period. This is why, whenever possible, make one vendor responsible for any improvements, upgrades, or repairs on the system. This allows you to develop a rapport with the vendor, makes it easier and quicker to obtain parts for the system, and the vendor is only a phone call away if there are any specific questions or training needs. Having only one vendor is more cost effective and makes it easier to address and resolve any issues that are encountered with the system.

Figure 1.1 presents an example of an add-on that the leader of a security surveillance center project would submit to the vendor.

The security surveillance center is the nerve center of the security surveillance system. The role of today's operator in the modern security surveillance center is similar to that of a conductor of an orchestra. The security surveillance center operator is the maestro of the operation in relation to the tempo of which personnel are dispatched to scenes and incidents. The following are some of the ways that a security surveillance center operator can be informed of an incident:

- Someone calls by telephone.
- Someone calls over the radio.
- Observations are made by the operator on the CCTV system.
- Someone physically makes notification.

To be successful, the security surveillance center operator must be part of a complete safety and security plan that contains intrusion detection, video assessment,

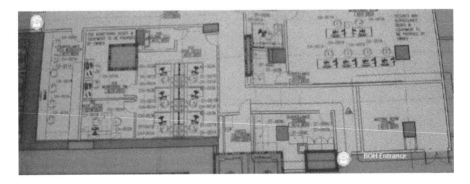

FIGURE 1.1 Security surveillance center add-on – ID telephone and door release for security surveillance center.

fire detection, access control, and full two-way communication that has an uninterrupted power supply (UPS). The most significant reason that the role of the security surveillance center operator has come to light in recent years, and the importance of professionalism of those who are involved in the realm of the security surveillance center, has been the worldwide increase in theft, terrorism, and the need to protect people and assets. The use of state-of-the-art security surveillance systems will have relatively little impact if the security surveillance center operator is not fully trained and knowledgeable. It is of paramount importance that this position be adequately trained and kept abreast of modern technology and events that could have a negative impact on the operation or on others.

The modern security surveillance center operator should be competent, knowledgeable, and have a skill set that includes

- Knowledge of security surveillance center duties and responsibilities
- Ability to remain calm under pressure
- Ability to communicate clearly, concisely, and accurately
- Knowledge of the intricacies of the CCTV system
- Knowledge of key control
- Knowledge of alarm types and responses
- Knowledge of the fire command system
- Knowledge of emergency procedures
- Knowledge of procedures for notifying emergency services and law enforcement
- Ability to recognize signs of when guests or employees may be involved in illegal, suspicious, or improper activity

The duties and responsibilities of the security surveillance center operator include the following:

- Relieve prior security surveillance center operators of all duties and responsibilities and account for equipment. Ascertain what occurred during the previous shift that might be relevant to, or affect, the oncoming shift's operation.
- Ensure the relief of personnel from the previous shift, staffing shortage is noted and recorded and a representative of the security surveillance center leadership team is notified.
- Advise any personnel, whose assignments were affected, of any correction, addition, or changes in posting as a result of the information supplied by the previous shift.
- Maintain a daily summary sheet of all security surveillance center–related activities including but not limited to responses to alarms, accidents, incidents, and investigations involving patrons and employees.
- Dispatch and maintain accountability of radios and equipment assigned to security surveillance center personnel.
- Record all daily paperwork including the posting assignments sheets with changes, corrections, and additions.

- Maintain the key control book, to include the issuing, receiving, and physical security of all keys assigned to the security surveillance center.
- Make notifications, via telephone, prior to any significant escort including armor car delivery or as directed by a representative of the security surveillance center leadership team.
- Monitor all security surveillance center alarms, and direct responses to appropriate personnel to any activated alarm.
- Monitor all equipment in the security surveillance center.
- Maintain control of, provide direction, and coordinate all radio traffic related to security surveillance center operations.
- Maintain control of all security surveillance center telephone communications.
- Assist security surveillance center personnel to become more effective and efficient.
- All security surveillance center paperwork is to be organized, accurate and completed in a timely manner by the end of the shift.
- Advise the oncoming shift of any pertinent information regarding incidents, investigations, alarms, and so on, that could impact the oncoming shift's operation.
- The CCTV system will be monitored to ensure the safety of the property, company assets, and the safety and security of the internal and external guests.
- Telephone calls should be answered by the security surveillance center with proper etiquette (i.e., "Good morning."/"Good afternoon."/"Good evening." Thank you for calling the security surveillance center. This is _____. How may I assist you?).
- Any communications received that are deemed to be important to the security surveillance center are to be reported to the proper personnel and logged into the daily shift activity report (police, fire rescue, bomb threats, etc.), and a representative of the security surveillance center leadership team is to be notified immediately.
- When CCTV coverage is needed by law enforcement or others, security surveillance center personnel will review it, store it, and burn a DVD of the activities pertaining to the incident. Prior to release to law enforcement, etc., all paperwork will be completed and signed by the person accepting the DVD and the member of the security surveillance center leadership team issuing the DVD.
- When a priority fire alarm is received on the life safety system in the security surveillance center, security surveillance center personnel must immediately acknowledge and then notify the proper personnel to check the location that is displayed on the panel. Once the location is checked and reported to be clear, the security surveillance center operator will reset the system.
- When an armored car comes for pickups or deliveries, the security surveillance center operator will receive a phone call notifying the estimated time of arrival (ETA). The security surveillance operator will make notifications to the appropriate agencies and departments and advise of the ETA.

- Any information received by the security surveillance center deemed to be urgent, possibly impact the life and safety of others, deemed important, and so on, will be reported to the proper personnel, a member of the security surveillance center leadership team will be notified immediately, and the information will be logged. Examples of urgent information includes contact involving the following:
  - Police
  - Fire rescue
  - Bomb threats
- Complete other security surveillance center tasks as assigned by member of the security surveillance leadership team.

The proper relief and shift change of the security surveillance center should include the following:

- At the beginning of each shift, the oncoming security surveillance center personnel will be briefed by the outgoing shift.
- The outgoing and incoming shifts are to make sure the security surveillance center is clean, trash is emptied, and all paperwork is completed.
- All logs and forms are to be properly completed.
- Outgoing personnel will prepare all reports, conduct a camera check, and record on the camera log all discrepancies and advise the oncoming shift of any pertinent information.
- Outgoing and incoming personnel will check all systems, including the fire command center, life safety systems, and so on, to ensure all are in working order. Any discrepancies will be immediately reported to a member of the security surveillance center leadership team.

The goal of any security surveillance center is to be able to positively identify subjects involved in incidents, committing crime, or violating policy and procedures. The three main reasons the security surveillance center uses CCTV are to:

- Witness what is happening.
- Record what has happened.
- Act as a deterrent.

The following are the three levels of resolution that are obtained from the CCTV system with a minimum of recommended levels of lighting measured in foot candles (fc) and the percentage of the scene the object should occupy. The following levels are dependent on the camera resolution, size, and proximity of the object:

- *Detection*: the ability to detect the presence of an object in an area of interest. The ability to detect there is something versus nothing.
  - 0.5 foot candle (fc).
  - Each scene should stand on its own merit.

- *Classification or recognition*: increased resolution provides sufficient information to determine what is present by class and the ability to recognize what type of thing it is (person, animal, car, etc.):
  - 1 foot candle (fc).
  - Object is 10% of scene (6 foot subject would occupy a minimum of 10% of the screen).
- *Identification*: improved resolution sufficient to uniquely identify an object on the basis of details of appearance, specific features, or details; the ability to identify a specific individual from other people:
  - 2 foot candle (fc).
  - Object is 20% of the scene (6 foot subject would occupy a minimum of 20% of the screen).

Security surveillance centers provide multiple functions in the overall security plan and provide asset protection by monitoring the activities of personnel and guests. The security surveillance center operator detects many types of activity with the CCTV system, including

- Perimeter activity
- Unwanted entry
- Suspicious activities
- Criminal activities

The utilization of CCTV works well alone but becomes more robust when used in conjunction with other technologies. One such technology is intrusion-detection alarm devices, such as door sensors, which when activated report the location of an event to the security surveillance center. When received, the security surveillance center dispatches personnel to the scene to investigate in conjunction with manually searching the CCTV system in an attempt to locate and view the event area prior to the arrival of responding personnel. This can be cumbersome at times and sometimes may not be possible.

A safer option is to coordinate the use of intrusion detection devices, such as door sensors, with video motion detection to alert the security surveillance center that an intrusion has occurred. The application of these technological pieces works best when a specific camera is dedicated and programmed, such as a PTZ CCTV camera, to automatically provide coverage of the area any time an intrusion detection device, or door sensor, is activated. When received, the security surveillance center is able to view the event and take the appropriate action without jeopardizing the safety of the responders. When implementing this strategy, it is important to ensure that CCTV coverage is not compromised when the PTZ camera rotates to the predetermined location in reaction to the activation of other sensors or devices designed to initiate the movement of the PTZ. In order to eliminate this type of situation a fixed camera can be installed at these locations.

Another method of combining technology with the security surveillance center is the combination of emergency call boxes with a CCTV system. When the push button is activated on the emergency call box, an immediate voice communication is established with the security surveillance center, which specifies the location in conjunction with a video image of the subject at the call box. With this power of synergy and utilizing technology effectively and efficiently, the security surveillance center has the capability to quickly evaluate a situation and swiftly take appropriate action.

For those establishments that have elevators, the following system could be implemented to provide the utmost care and safety for those who operate and use the elevator. An emergency call button should be clearly marked inside of the elevator that, when activated, provides the user with immediate voice communication with the security surveillance center. A fixed CCTV camera should be installed between the ceiling and the wall in the back corner of the elevator facing toward the elevator doors. When the emergency button is activated, the security surveillance center is able to immediately speak with and observe the subject who activated the alarm and take appropriate action.

As discussed, security surveillance systems are most effective when integrated with other security hardware and procedures to form a coherent unit. When combined, the total security surveillance center is more robust than the individual stand-alone systems. The implementation of synergetic security surveillance systems enables the security surveillance center to reduce the reaction time to evaluate an event and respond appropriately. These systems provide security surveillance centers reliable and timely information that assists in determining if an incident is a nonevent, the location of the subject involved, or if assistance is needed.

The previously listed examples are just a few ways technology acts as a force multiplier by allowing the roles of many to be completed by a few. For example, as previously described, the use of the security surveillance center allows the event to be immediately monitored and evaluated without jeopardizing the safety of the responders. Also, if needed, simultaneous notification to emergency services by the security surveillance center is available.

This force multiplier and synergy effect make for compelling arguments to administrators and the leaders of any organization to support and improve current security surveillance center programs or to implement security surveillance center systems at properties where they do not currently exist. The proper use of security surveillance center systems has a positive impact on the ROI by acting as a force multiplier by enabling coverage of areas without increasing, or decreasing, the workforce. Security surveillance center systems adequately protect internal and external guests; reduce theft; save lives; save money; enable the monitoring of remote sites; increase the coverage of and protection of a facility for a relatively low capital investment and minimal operational costs; and aid in the detection of internal incidents, external incidents, and criminal activity.

THE BADGE CONTROL COMPONENT OF THE SECURITY SURVEILLANCE CENTER

Many times the purpose of security surveillance center personnel is to verify and control access to the facility by the issuance, tracking, and collection of access badges into controlled areas of the property. The following are the types of badges that the security surveillance center is responsible for maintaining, tracking, and destroying:

- Employee temporary access badge
- Nonemployee temporary access badge
- Vendor temporary access badge
- Contractor temporary access badge

Requestors of temporary badges will report to the security surveillance center badging area and request a temporary badge. A member of the security surveillance center team will include the following when a request is received:

- Contact the immediate department leader of the employee requesting the badge and verify employment.
- If unable to confirm with the requestor's immediate department leader, a member of the security surveillance center leadership team will be contacted to verify employment.
- If the requestor is not actively employed, access badge will not be issued.
- Inform the requestor to call his or her supervisor or department that he or she wishes to access and schedule an appointment.
- If the requestor is actively employed, confirm his or her identification, request to see picture ID.
- If identification is confirmed, a temporary access badge should be issued to the area(s) the requestor is authorized to have access to.
- Advise the requestor that the access badge must be displayed at all times and that the badge must be returned to the security surveillance center upon exiting the property.
- The following information will be documented into the access badge log:
  - Date issued
  - Time issued
  - Requestor's first name, last name, and employee number
  - Authorized by—first and last name
  - Location to be accessed
  - Position
  - Issuing security surveillance center personnel first name, last name, and employee number

THE KEY CONTROL COMPONENT OF THE SECURITY SURVEILLANCE CENTER

The purpose of the key control system is to ensure accountability for all keys maintained and controlled by the security surveillance center. All keys controlled by the security surveillance center for storage and issuance should be secured in a lockable container within the security surveillance center. Access to the key storage container should be limited to designated security surveillance center leaders and their designees. The maintenance of the keys should be kept by using a bound ledger book. To ensure the continuity of the keys, the following information should be recorded in the key control log:

- Key number or name
- Date and time key is signed out
- Signature and employee number of the person receiving key
- Name and employee number of the issuing security surveillance center operator
- Signature and employee number of employee returning key
- Signature and employee number of security surveillance center operator receiving key
- Date and time key returned

The security surveillance center operator should do the following if an entry is made into the key control log in error:

Using a red pen, the error should be voided by drawing a single line through the entry, placing their initials next to the voided entry, and making the corrected entry on the next available line. In no case should white-out or erasers be used to correct an entry made in error. It should be the responsibility of the incoming security surveillance center operator to ensure that all keys are accounted for at the beginning of the shift. This verification will be completed before the outgoing security surveillance center operator leaves the area. In the event that a key is found to be missing, a member of the security surveillance center leadership team must be notified immediately.

Keys issued from the security surveillance center should not be passed from shift to shift by the users. At the change of shift, within the various departments, the department users should be required to sign the issued keys in/out with the security surveillance center operators. This process will ensure the perpetual accountability of the keys.

Generally, properties use the following three types of keys:

- *Restricted*: are generally money-related keys that should be retained under the strictest conditions. A technological solution is a computerized key access system that utilizes a badge swipe and fingerprint and requires at least one other person to release the key. Restricted keys are generally money-related keys.
- *Unrestricted*: are generally non-money-related keys. These keys should be retained in a lockable key cabinet located in the security surveillance center. Access to the key box should be limited to personnel of the security surveillance center.
- *Company keys*: are generally office and storage room keys.

ALARM TYPE AND RESPONSE COMPONENT OF THE SECURITY SURVEILLANCE CENTER

TYPES OF ALARMS

- *Door (intrusion)*: This type of alarm is activated when alarmed doors have been opened. Examples include the perimeter doors or entrance doors to stores.
- *Panic*: This alarm is a push-button alarm that employees will use for hold-ups, disturbances, thefts, medical emergencies, and any other situation that warrants an immediate response.

MALFUNCTIONS

The facility department has the responsibility of servicing and repairing the security alarm system. In the event of a total alarm malfunction, the facilities department will consider this a priority. In the event of a complete alarm malfunction, it will be the responsibility of the department leader to inform the employees of their areas of their responsibilities. As an added protection, the security surveillance center will dispatch personnel to the location and place the area under observation of the CCTV system.

PANIC (HOLDUP) AND ROBBERY

When large sums of money are in circulation on the premises of a property, there will always exist the possibility that holdup or robbery attempts will occur. A holdup and robbery involves the use of force to obtain anything of value. The force may be direct or implied. A weapon may be shown or the person may indicate that he or she has a weapon. Whenever this occurs, it must be assumed that a weapon is being used. Employees must not resist.

Cashiers should comply with the below listed instructions when a robbery takes place:

- All points of sale (POSs) should have holdup alarms available. The alarm button should be activated discreetly and when danger no longer exists.
- Pay attention to the events taking place. Remember the physical characteristics of the person. Listen to the person's voice, remain calm, and keep any written demand for money. Witnesses should not converse with each other or with any other person (could be comparing notes), unless they are responsible for having control over the crime scene.
- The employee involved in the situation must notify a member of the departmental leadership team as soon as possible. Employees must safeguard the area, not allowing anyone into the crime scene until the appropriate personnel arrive on scene. Nothing should be touched. Upon arrival the crime scene will be turned over to law enforcement.
- When a panic (holdup) alarm is received, the security surveillance center will observe the live view of the location and surrounding area on the CCTV system. Appropriate personnel will be contacted. Personnel responding to

the alarm must use caution and be aware of their surroundings. If an actual panic (holdup) situation has taken place, notify the security surveillance center and/or a representative of the security surveillance center leadership team immediately. Treat the incident as a crime scene.

- If the alarm is not a panic (holdup) alarm, malfunction, or mistake, responding personnel will via radio announce the alarm malfunction, then telephone the security surveillance center to report the alarm malfunction.
- The security surveillance center monitors the panic (holdup) alarms that are located in cash-handling areas, POSs, and high-risk areas.
- The security surveillance center monitors door alarms located throughout the property. An inspection of the alarms should take place frequently. This inspection should be conducted to ensure that all systems are functioning properly. Any discrepancies will be noted on the alarm inspection form and be corrected immediately.

The emergency procedures and response component of the security surveillance centers is a critical component of the emergency procedures of any organization, regardless of the size. When an emergency or crisis is developing or is at its peak, all involved constantly contact the security surveillance center for updates. This information is combined with other information and details to determine if a formal command center is needed. Until a final determination is made or established, the security surveillance center should assume the duties and function of a command center. Even when a command center is operational, the security surveillance center plays an important role in any emergency or antiterrorist plan by protecting human life by viewing remote locations, viewing firsthand what and where things are happening, prioritizing emergency responses, determining if any additional emergencies are in progress, and when normalcy has been achieved marking the end of the crisis or emergency.

Since the reaction time to an emergency, fire, or other disaster is critical, it is very important for the security surveillance center to view and report the status of an incident location to responding personnel before they arrive on scene. Being the eyes of the emergency scene or crisis allows the security surveillance center to send the appropriate reaction team with adequate equipment to provide an optimum response. In the event of a fire, when sprinkler heads activate or a fire sensor goes into alarm, the security surveillance center can quickly ascertain if the event is an alarm malfunction, minor crisis, or major event. This prior viewing of the actual scene can save lives and reduce damage and asset losses.

The security surveillance center plays a crucial role in the overall security plan. During any event—disaster, crisis, theft, or emergency—the security surveillance center provides information to the responding personnel. Based on the information received from the security surveillance center, the personnel respond, react, and take action according to the information received. The security surveillance center monitors the scene and responders for any escalation of the situation, like a big brother standing in the shadows. The security surveillance center "watches the backs" of those responding and the parties involved and, if warranted, makes notifications for assistance for additional personnel, emergency services, or law enforcement.

In April 2011, the color-coded Homeland Security Advisory System (HSAS) was replaced with the National Terrorism Advisory System (NTAS). The NTAS goal is to effectively communicate information about terrorist threats by providing timely, detailed information to many key areas, including the private sector. Each alert provides information about a threat including geographic region; mode of transportation; critical infrastructure potentially affected by the threat; actions being taken by authorities; and steps that can be taken to help prevent, mitigate, or respond to the threat. The NTAS alerts are based on the nature of the threat: in some cases, alerts will be sent directly to law enforcement or affected areas of the private sector.

There are two types of alerts issued by the NTAS: Imminent Threat Alert and Elevated Threat Alert. The Imminent Threat Alert warns of a credible, specific, and impending terrorist threat against the United States. The Elevated Threat Alert warns of a credible terrorist threat against the United States. These alerts will include a clear statement that there is an imminent threat or an elevated threat. The alerts provide a concise summary of the potential threat, information about actions being taken to ensure public safety, and recommended steps that can be taken to help prevent, mitigate, or respond to the threat.

The alerts issued by the NTAS have a sunset provision, which is an individual threat alert issued for a specific time period and scheduled to automatically expire. It may be extended if new information becomes available or the threat evolves.

The sunset provision indicates a specific date when the alert expires—there no longer will be a constant NTAS alert or blanket warning that there is an overarching threat. If threat information changes for an alert, the Secretary of Homeland Security may announce an updated NTAS alert. All changes, including the announcement that cancels an NTAS alert, are distributed the same way as the original alert.

The following is a sample of a heightened security alert program that should be implemented in the event of an escalated alert from the NTAS. The following should also be implemented if the security surveillance center is in receipt of credible information received from law enforcement pertaining to a terrorist or any other type of activity that presents a real and present danger to the lives and safety of employees, guests, and visitors.

HEIGHTENED SECURITY SURVEILLANCE CENTER ALERT PROCEDURES

The purpose of this heightened security procedure is to increase security awareness in the event the NTAS issues an Imminent Threat Alert or Elevated Threat Alert. The heightened security alert procedure should also be used based on world conditions or information received by actual law enforcement intelligence of terrorist activities or other types of activities that could jeopardize the safety of employees, guests, visitors, and the property. Prior to implementing this procedure, a meeting should be conducted with the key leaders and decision-makers of the property—usually the executive team. The nature and type of alert or threat should be discussed and the actions taken should be agreed upon and implemented. There should also be predetermined follow-up meetings to discuss any updates pertaining to the threat or alert. This procedure is designed to phase-in as the perceived level of risk assessment increases. The heightened security procedures are as follows:

1. *Building Exterior Perimeter*
   a. The security surveillance center in addition to vehicles, bikes, and so on, will maintain a constant patrol of the perimeter of the building.
   b. No vehicle should be allowed to stop and/or park along the curb line adjacent to the building.
   c. All delivery trucks should be stopped to examine the delivery bill of lading prior to entry into the building and/or dock areas.
   d. Perimeter patrols should ensure all emergency exits remain closed and secure.
2. *Valet/Special Parking Areas*
   a. Signs should be posted indicating that the insides of vehicles, trunks, and cargo areas are subject to inspection before vehicles will be accepted for valet or special parking privileges.
   b. The security surveillance center will patrol key areas using the CCTV system, and personnel will be positioned at key areas such as in valet areas or in the designated vehicle drop-off area to conduct inspections of those vehicles dropped off by customers or being parked in special areas.
   c. Any person arriving who does not wish his or her vehicle to be inspected will be requested to park off site.
   The following is a valet/special parking sign example:

Attention: Valet and Special Parking Areas

For your safety and security, all vehicles are subject to a visual security inspection of the interior, trunk, and/or cargo areas prior to using the valet or special parking areas. Those not willing to have the inspection take place, please utilize other-parking areas.

3. *Building Interior Perimeter*
   a. The security surveillance center will patrol the area using the CCTV system, and personnel will establish a back-of-house perimeter patrol to screen for unauthorized individuals.
   b. Credentials will be verified and employee status of anyone in the back-of-house areas who is not displaying the proper credentials will be confirmed.
4. *Loading Docks (After Normal Operating Hours)*
   To prevent unauthorized access, the security surveillance center will patrol the area using the CCTV system, and personnel will be assigned to patrol the loading dock after hours when the dock is not normally in use.
5. *Entrance Control*
   Depending on the type of threat and suspected activity, the security surveillance center will patrol the area using the CCTV system, and personnel

will be assigned to patrol the entrances to ensure no large bags, backpacks, briefcases, and so on, are permitted on the premises.

6. *Controlling Property Access Roads*

For an extra layer of protection, the security surveillance center will patrol the area using the CCTV system, and personnel will be assigned to posts and conduct patrols of the main access roads leading into the property from public roadways. Visual inspections are to be conducted, and all unusual or suspicious activity is to be immediately reported to the security surveillance center leadership team.

The following is an example of the implementation of these procedures. These are general guidelines and, if necessary, should be modified to meet the specific individual needs of a property.

1. Intelligence information is received from law enforcement that warns of a credible threat.

Implement Sections I, II, and III.

2. Intelligence information is received from law enforcement that indicates that there is a credible, specific, and impending threat.

Implement Sections I, II, III, IV, V, and VI.

To conclude this chapter, the following is a 51-point checklist that I have compiled over the decades during the opening of various properties. The size of the properties ranged from millions of dollars to billions of dollars, and the locations have ranged from coast to coast of the United States and areas in between. The weight of each of the items in the checklist depends on the amenities of the property, the size of the property, and the stage of completion during which one becomes involved in the opening of a property. The items in the checklist are not in any particular order—the order of importance depends on the stage of completion of the project in which one finds himself or herself. Regardless of the phase of completion, it is a good idea to verify that the items listed below are scheduled to be done, have been completed, or will be completed prior to the opening of any property.

1. Determine staffing needs. Obtain an overview layout of property to determine post-assignments and full-time equivalent (FTE) levels. Personally, I prefer to color-coordinate and identify each position on the overview layout of the property into the following categories:
   a. 24/7 positions: posts that will require coverage 24 hours a day/7 days a week
   b. High-volume positions: posts that will require coverage during high-volume days (e.g., Friday, Saturday, and Sunday)
   Once this is completed, it helps to provide an overview of the departmental needs. This makes it easier to explain the staffing needs of the department to others.
2. Review plans/layout to determine crime prevention through environmental design (CPTED) features in the design phase—many times implementing CPTED features in the post-construction phase can be very costly.

3. Plan CCTV layout and design. Review the layout and design with vendors to ensure conduit, wire, cameras, and equipment meet the needs and specs requested. One way to ensure everyone is on the same page is to identify and spray-paint on the concrete floor the location of where PTZ and fixed cameras will be installed overhead (prior to the permanent flooring being installed).

4. Make sure that the areas that are going to store sensitive computer and CCTV equipment, like the intermediate distribution framework (IDF) closest, have sufficient air conditioning to keep this equipment cool. Conduct and review calculations used to determine this to ensure they are accurate. In the event that the calculations were incorrect, temporary cooling units can be rented and used to keep the room cool until the issue is resolved.

5. Make sure that the construction security provides layers of protection. For example, badges must be displayed at all times and a hologram sticker, or similar identifier, should be issued and affixed to badges to gain entry to sensitive or protected areas. Adhere to a strict policy of no badge/no entry.

6. Review the life safety, fire suppression systems, and so on, to ensure that the addressing of the system is in real language and areas, alarms, and so on, are not identified by codes, numbers. Make sure the vendor who installed the system sets this up prior and tests prior to the property opening. The names on the addresses should be reviewed and determined by the leader of the security surveillance center.

7. Review traffic flow, garage, and destination signage to ensure all are accurate. Many times the initial installation of the signage can be conflicting and could cause major issues if not fixed prior to an opening of a property. Also make sure there is adequate CCTV coverage of the key areas of these locations.

8. Review the CCTV coverage in the elevators, hotel floors, and areas where guests may be processed for incidents that occur on the property. It is a good idea to install signage indicating that the area is monitored by a CCTV system.

9. Ensure that the fire suppression system for areas that store electronics like CCTV and IT systems do not have water sprinklers installed, but have fire suppression systems similar to the FM200.

10. Review the locations of automated external defibrillator (AED) units. If possible have an alarm go to dispatch when a door is opened, along with a local alarm.

11. Make sure to order all of your supplies (like operating supplies and equipment [OSE] and furniture, fixtures, and equipment [FFE]) with plenty of lead time. Remember if you are opening a property everything down to paper clips has to be ordered.

12. Review the bids on projects and ensure that guidelines are followed for RFPs, sole source, and the bidding process. Keep focused on the project and avoid the pitfalls.

13. Review the staffing, background process, and methodology utilized to hire. Make sure that the hiring of the team does not fall behind the predetermined time table. Remember to calculate the time needed to train when determining the time table for new hires.

14. Review the types of technology and equipment available to act as a force multiplier (i.e., patrol vehicles, bikes, other motorized vehicles, moveable towers to view parking areas, etc.).

15. Conduct a review of all employees' scheduling by every half hour for all 7 days to determine if there is enough onsite parking for employees and guests. If not, then a plan that would include shuttles, off-site parking, and so on, will need to be established.

16. Review the electronic report-writing software system to ensure that it meets the needs of the department and company.

17. Establish and review the standard operating procedures (SOPs).

18. If installing equipment, store it in a central area and bring it out as needed. Equipment should be inspected, cross-referenced with an Excel spreadsheet that lists all items, and numbered. There should be "yes" and "no" columns under the heading of damage, with another area to list the damage. For those entering any sensitive area, a sticker of the day or week should be implemented and displayed on a badge or a helmet. Those entering the zone should have to sign in and sign out.

19. A "see something, say something" program should be implemented in conjunction with a "just doesn't look right" (JDLR) roving patrol utilizing physical patrols and the security surveillance center.

20. Review the money storage area and armor car route, including armor car pick-up and drop-off points. There should be wire fencing on the ceiling and walls in conjunction with other ceiling and wall material to make it more difficult to access. Alarms and motion sensors should also be installed in the ceiling space, entrances, and exits.

21. If a property has mantraps, conduct a walk-through to review how they are designed to work and how they actually work. This can be one area where confusion occurs between the vendors and the end users. In my past experiences, I discovered that this area could work fine one day, as designed, and not work properly the next day due to unauthorized modifications. This is a crucial area and should be checked frequently to ensure that it works as designed.

22. Determine the location where and process by which a guest can retrieve lost and found items and address safety and security concerns.

23. Determine who controls the fire command center (FCC). This should be part of the security surveillance center because the area has the FCC panel, CCTV, and is the central point for communications.

24. If using an electronic key system, determine access properties for the accessibility of keys. How many employees and departments need to access a key—one, two, or three? The more sensitive the key, a greater number of employees or departments will be needed. Access levels fall into the following categories: single access, double access, and triple access.

25. If the property is equipped with a parking garage, determine the maximum vehicle height that can enter and travel within the structure. Ensure that adequate signage is installed, notifying the operators of vehicles that are too high to enter the garage so that they can take an alternate route. Keep in mind that some emergency vehicles may have a vehicle height that is too high to enter the parking garage. In this circumstance, where vehicles are too high to enter the parking garage, a contingency plan will need to be developed.

26. If the property has valet parking, make sure an adequate amount of valet tickets are ordered and have a disclaimer on them regarding damage to vehicles must be reported prior to departing property. Verify if an electronic valet parking system is going to be utilized and that there is adequate CCTV coverage.

27. Determine what areas have an Uninterrupted Power Supply (UPS). The security surveillance center and life safety systems should have them.

28. Determine the location of duress alarms, and ensure all who work in the area are properly trained.

29. Establish and communicate a phone number and e-mail address where theft and other loss prevention issues can be anonymously reported.

30. All calls to 911 from any guest phone should have dual notification to the security surveillance center and emergency services.

31. Have the first digit on outside calls be anything but 9. Since nonlocal calls would require the dialing of 9-1 and then the area code. This will help to prevent accidental calls to 9-1-1.

32. All 911 calls should ID to the security surveillance center from all areas. They should indicate where the call was placed with a specific location, room number, and so on.

33. Meet with outside agencies such as the fire and police departments to review SOPs and emergency procedures. Discuss and address any concerns and have a department representative sign off when issued copies of documents.

34. If the property has an armored car delivery route, walk the primary and secondary routes. For example, at one property, I opened the initial plan was proposed prior to my arrival, and it had a route that went onto an elevator and exited into a sensitive cash-handling area where no one was authorized to be in the room except for the employees counting cash. Obviously I revised the route. This is an example of why it is important to be hands-on and review everything.

35. If there are other types of drops or delivery routes of important items, make sure to walk the drops and routes.

36. Review the locations of any AED units, emergency call boxes, CCTV cameras, and lighting. All of these items play a role in guests feeling safe and secure, which is a key reason why guests visit a property.

37. Conduct a time analysis for the amount of time that it will take guests to enter or exit a property for events. Some areas that may need to be addressed are parking garage flow, traffic flow, and surface parking areas.

38. If there are elevators on the property, the wait times during peak hours and during events should be evaluated. Elevator operators may need to be placed into the elevator to run express routes to certain levels.

39. Establish and communicate a muster point or points in the event that the property needs to be evacuated. Establish protocol to be followed in determining if all are safely accounted for.
40. Prior to opening, have a mock opening or dress rehearsal with preplanned exercises to ensure all are knowledgeable and properly trained for their positions and areas of responsibility.
41. Prior to the opening, communicate with other departments and areas to determine radio needs, shuttles, and so on, for the opening. Once determined, review with the leadership team for approval to next additional equipment.
42. If a massive job fair is planned, ensure that there is an adequate supply of water, AED units, portable toilets, umbrellas, traffic controllers, and so on. Advise local emergency service departments, such as the police, fire department, ambulance services of the event.
43. Review access control points and ensure that there are layers of protection and the area has a robust access control program.
44. Review and confirm final designs of property to ensure changes have not been made that would require the establishment of additional posts. Also ensure that key locations have not been modified or changed (i.e., the employee entrance, etc.).
45. Review and confirm that all uniforms have been ordered and that all members of the team have been issued properly fitting uniforms prior to opening.
46. Ensure that documented training for the entire team is completed prior to opening. Even the best training cannot cover every specific incident. For example, at one property I opened, the façade of a parking garage became unsecured and fell off narrowly missing an officer and crushing a guest vehicle. Fortunately no one was injured.
47. Many times the permanent sidewalks are installed after 3 to 6 months after the opening of a property, dictated by the trails that are made by the path people walk. Review these walkways and add CCTV if needed.
48. Establish a centralized badge control access, request, and distribution area. Usually this is part of the security surveillance center.
49. Ensure that immediately after the opening ceremony/event that everything is cleared out and the normal operation of the property begins.
50. For the opening ceremony/event, ensure that there is an adequate supply of water, AED units, paramedics, law enforcement, portable toilets, umbrellas, traffic controllers, and so on. Advise local emergency service departments like the police, fire department, ambulance services, etc., of the event.
51. Have fun!

2 Overview of the Control Room and Console Design

The proper design of the security surveillance center console and room is one of the most critical components of the security surveillance center. The location and console design are important factors to the overall success of the operation of the security surveillance center. For example, many times in smaller properties, in a hotel and hospitality environment, the security surveillance center may be located in an area that has a direct view of the main entrance of the property, and all the doors providing access to the lobby area are controlled remotely.

This type of design is usually reserved for when only the lobby entrance is the authorized after-hours entrance and exit point. The size of the security surveillance center does not always correspond to the size of the property. For example, if only one operator is assigned in the center that has an abundance of equipment, the operator would not be able to handle the equipment efficiently. When this type of situation is encountered, staffing levels should be evaluated to determine if an increase in staffing is needed.

Typically, staffing the security surveillance center with one operator on a 24/7 basis would require an absolute bare minimum of 4.2 Full Time Equivalents (FTEs). This number is derived by performing the following calculation. 24 hours a day multiplied by 7 days a week equals 168 hours. 168 hours is divided by 40 hours which equals 4.2. ($24 \times 7 = 168$, $168/40 = 4.2$). This does not take vacation time, etc., into consideration. To accommodate for vacations, sick leave, etc., would usually require a minimum of 4.5 FTE's needed to cover a post 24/7. At many times the security surveillance operator works behind protective windows with a deal-tray similar to those utilized at bank teller windows. This provides security surveillance center personnel a safe, effective, and easy way to issue and/or exchange badges, keys, and identification.

The location of the security surveillance center is best designed to have easy access and egress for emergency personnel, first responders, law enforcement officials, and the fire department. Any doors leading into the area should be monitored by a closed-circuit television (CCTV) system, and access should be controlled remotely by security surveillance center personnel. Keep in mind that each security surveillance center is unique depending on the needs of the facility and the philosophy of the leadership of the facility or company.

At a minimum, the security surveillance center should consist of a CCTV system that has the ability to expand into other areas of the operation, such as key control, badge control, monitoring alarms, and so on. As simple as this may sound, the security surveillance center should have a quality color copier. I have been amazed over the years at the number of times that I have had to explain and justify why this is such a vital component of this area. One reason, which usually always tips the discussion for the purchase, is that a quality color printer is needed to quickly print out and distribute photos of persons of interest to key areas and personnel should a critical situation be encountered.

Another area of importance, depending on the size of the organization, departments, etc., is to have a specific area where the review of CCTV coverage can be viewed without compromising security surveillance center information and ongoing investigations. In my experiences, I have found that having a room outside of the security surveillance center is the best location to install a CCTV review room for other departments to review coverage. How the process should work is that the security surveillance center receives a call from a department leader requesting a review of an area for any CCTV coverage pertaining to an incident or violation. After the review is conducted, the requestor should be contacted and advised of the status of the review. If coverage does exist, the requestor should be invited to the review room where security surveillance center personnel prepare the footage for review on a monitor in the review room. Security surveillance center personnel then grant access to the review room and have the requester sign in on the visitor log, which includes name, date, time, department, reason, signature, and identification number. Security surveillance center personnel then go over what the CCTV footage revealed with the requestor. When the review is complete, the visitor signs out on the visitor log with the time of departure from the review room. In the event that CCTV coverage is not sufficient to make a determination regarding the request, the response to the inquiry for coverage should be that the coverage is conclusive.

Because electronics are a vital component of the operation of a security surveillance center, it is important not to have it located in an area below ground level or susceptible to flooding. Many times the security surveillance center expert may not be consulted during the construction of a project until after the building designs have been approved and the physical layout has been built.

Believe it or not, the following is a true story regarding the location of a security surveillance center on a property that was on an island. I will not divulge the year, name, or location, because the intent of this example is to be used as a lesson learned and not to embarrass anyone. To make a long story short, the security surveillance center was located in the basement of a very large property. When severe weather struck the island, the basement flooded and you can guess what happened from there—I will let you fill in the rest of the story. Needless to say, there was a disruption in business and a lot of finger pointing. This is an example of why it is important to have the leader of a security surveillance center involved in the early construction stages of any project to review the plans, make suggestions, and consult with the leaders driving the project.

Many times the security surveillance center performs many functions at the same time and is located at the entrance area of a building or area that it is protecting. As previously explained, it should not be located below ground level or in an area that has a chance of flooding. If the security surveillance center is located in a main entry point or reception area, entry into the CCTV component of the security surveillance center should be controlled by an access control system with a camera monitoring the security surveillance center door. This will give the ability to the personnel in the security surveillance center to view who is attempting to access the area and permit only authorized personnel into the security surveillance center. Regardless of the location of the security surveillance center, the door should remain closed and locked at all times and should be made of reinforced material.

When developing or updating the CCTV system of a security surveillance center, it is important not only to design it for the current needs and uses but to also have a vision of the future areas and projects of the facility that are under development that will need additional coverage and support from the security surveillance center. It is important to build and develop the CCTV system so that it has the capability to be easily expanded as the needs of a property grow. This may be relatively expensive, and a large amount of money may have to be spent on the front end of the project. But in the long run, the forward thinking and planning will be beneficial for all involved and should result in the saving of money term.

Also it is important to remember when purchasing the software and hardware components of the security surveillance center that modern technology develops and changes at a very fast rate. If possible, do not purchase last year's technology at a "bargain price." This may work fine for the present but could quickly be outdated and not meet the future needs of the facility.

For example, not all software and hardware are created equal. When exploring the different options available regarding CCTV cameras and software, it is important to compare the type of coverage available of each. Take CCTV cameras for example. One camera may cost twice as much as another but may have the ability to provide four times the coverage. At first glance, if someone was unaware of the amount of coverage area of each camera, it would appear that the lower-priced camera was the better deal. However, once the coverage factor of each camera is examined and it is discovered that one of the more expensive cameras provides four times more coverage than the less expensive camera at twice the price of the less expensive camera, the decision should be an easy one. More coverage with less cameras at a better value would result in less cameras being needed and covering a larger area at less expense on the front end. Additional cost savings would be recognized in the areas of installation, maintenance, and so on, because of the fewer number of cameras involved in the project.

CCTV cameras and the software must have the capability to work well with each other and should be designed to provide video to specific users. Ideally the CCTV cameras and software selected are designed specifically for each other. However, many times, in an effort to reduce cost, the lowest priced product is purchased. When designing a CCTV system and control room, it is important to take into consideration the intended use of the system. For example, if the goal is security and crime prevention, then the goal is to create a psychological effect to act as a deterrent to crime and to identify criminals before, during, or after crimes occur by viewing live CCTV coverage or by reviewing recorded coverage. The CCTV system should be designed to include the monitoring of people, places, products, and areas where money transactions occur.

The difficult part may be explaining this clearly to the executive leadership, who are many times in the position of trying to reduce the expenses associated with projects such as this. The job of the leader of the security surveillance center is to clearly explain the benefits of the desired software and hardware of the system and why it is the best choice not only for the present but also for the growth and future needs of the property.

The following is a general overview of the components of the security surveillance center control room. The security surveillance center is the nerve center where the CCTV system is maintained and operated. The difference between CCTV and ordinary television is that ordinary television broadcasts its signal openly to the public, whereas CCTV is not transmitted to the public. CCTV systems are mainly used for security and surveillance purposes and have become very affordable and attainable so that almost anyone who has a business or an area that needs a CCTV system for security purposes can easily purchase one from a specialist, from a chain department store, or even online.

Depending on the complexity of the system, the components that make up a CCTV system include the following:

- *Cable*: Coaxial cable is used to connect wired CCTV, which is used to transmit and receive signals from the monitoring point.
- *Cameras* (Input): This is the most important component because it collects the images. The camera is the eyes of the system and is available in a variety of options, including wireless, wired, covert, fixed, pan-tilt-zoom (PTZ), waterproof, weatherproof, infrared, color, black and white.
  - Analog cameras basically work by the modulation and amplitude of linear frequencies. The storage and resolution do not change since the bandwidth used to deliver the image does not change. Analog cameras convert their signal to a digital format so that their image can be recorded onto a digital video recorder (DVR), usually through a piece of hardware located in the DVR or between the camera and the DVR. Analog cameras are actually fully digital inside as they contain a digital signal processor (DSP) that allows for various image processing technologies to be applied. Digital signal processing permits the images projected by the lens on the face of the charged coupled device (CCD) chip to be adjusted pixel by pixel to provide the best picture possible rather than, as in analog video processing, the application of an average value for brightness, contrast, or color. Although signal processing within the camera is digital, the most common way that it is transmitted is analog using coaxial cable.
  - IP video cameras produce an image and encode it for streaming over a network. This device combines a lens, imager, DSP, and digital-to-analog converter in a single package. The network video camera connects to the network and can be controlled remotely using a PTZ lens capability. The camera can be controlled by the commands sent from the security surveillance center personnel directly to the camera over the network.

- Video analytics does not merely record events; it has the ability to make decisions on when, where, who, and how to record. Video content analysis (VCA) is a subset of video analytics that analyzes the content of recordings. In my opinion, this is the most significant development in video surveillance systems to date. This allows a camera to detect and distinguish a target image from other types of images. For example, it has the ability to distinguish an intruder from a car, a flock of geese, and so on. Many times video analytics does not immediately perform effectively. However, once configured and "trained" to recognize its targets, it is a very effective tool.
- *Monitor*: Most regular televisions can be used as monitors. The main difference between regular televisions and CCTV monitors is that CCTV monitors do not need a tuner.
  - Analog system monitors are installed parallel to the recorders. The switch splits the video signal between the monitor and recorder.
  - Digital monitors, or systems using a virtual switch, allow viewing of whatever is sent to it by the software. This allows the monitor to view other cameras, playback, recorded video, and enhanced or multiple images created by the software while the live images are being recorded.
- *Multiplexers or splitting*: These allow for the recording of multiple cameras. In security surveillance centers, it is common for more than one video source to be monitored at the same time. A multiplexer allows multiple inputs to be displayed on a single monitor. A splitter allows a particular input to be sent to more than one monitor. A multiplexer can take signals from several cameras and display them on a single screen in a grid.
- *Controllers*: These manipulate the PTZ cameras.
- *Switchers*: These provide the ability to switch between cameras. They control the cameras and route signals to the recorders and monitors. The switch allows for more than one remote controller within the system. Ensure that the security surveillance center can override all others in the event of an important investigation or emergency.
- *Virtual switch*: Cameras go into the computer and the software assigns the cameras to monitor and record while providing remote control access.
- *Digital video recorder (DVR)*: A DVR is a multichannel device that acquires video images and stores data in a proprietary format on a non-removable hard disk. DVRs can record for an extended period of time depending on the size of the hard drive. When space becomes unavailable on the hard drive, footage may be erased to allow for the new data to be stored. Frame rate is an important factor: 1 frame per second (FPS) is considered choppy, and 30 FPS is considered smooth. The higher the FPS, the more storage space will be needed. It is not always necessary to use a higher FPS. For example, a view of a gate or door can be at a lower rate because the movement is less important than watching a point of sale (POS) location when a person is on the register and the movements are very important.

- *Time-stamp generators*: These are an important aspect of videos obtained by the security surveillance center. Camera images and those that are sent to a DVR superimpose the time and date on the image. It is important to ensure that the time and date are accurate to aid in investigations of policy violations or in those of a civil, legal, or criminal nature.
- *Video servers/encoder devices*: Video servers or encoder devices that use megapixel and progressive scan imaging make it easier to identify objects and individuals in recordings than it is for their nearest equivalent analog counterparts, assuming that the same imaging technologies are used and can be managed from any accessible location on the network. These are usually placed behind corporate firewalls and are not generally accessible to the public. If an IP video device is publicly accessible, the risks involve a denial of service since the IP video camera will only support a finite number of users. The use of Port Authentication Protocol (802.1x) aids in managing video streaming and accessibility of the recording and monitoring devices that exist directly on a corporate network.
- *IP video encoders*: These are often referred to as single-channel or multichannel video encoders or video servers; simply put, they convert video from analog cameras and allow it to be viewed on a network system.
- *Power sources*: The security surveillance center should have primary and secondary power sources. The secondary power source should consist of a battery backup or uninterrupted power supply (UPS) system and/or a generator system powered by fuel such as diesel or gasoline. This type of power source can last for many days if needed—as long as it has the fuel needed to operate. These systems should be checked and inspected periodically to ensure that they are operational and ready to be used in the event that the main power supply to the security surveillance center is interrupted.

There are manpower costs associated with the previously listed scenarios and the skilled and artful selection and determination of the best fit for the property falls on the shoulders of the leader of the security surveillance center. This should be discussed fully with the executive leadership of the property weighing the pros and cons of each. Only after key factors such as safety, prevention, detection, associated costs, and so on, have been fully vetted should a decision be made.

COMPONENTS OF CCTV SYSTEM

The four basic components of a security surveillance center CCTV system, which we will go into in more detail, are composed of the following:

- Camera (input)
- Camera signal to monitor or screen involving a switch (control)
- DVR (output)
- Monitor or screen (output)

CAMERA

When selecting the camera, it is important to consider the use and performance required for the application. When selecting the camera housings, it is best to select the most appropriate type of housing depending on where each camera is to be installed. Pan-tilt heads and lenses may also be required depending on the mounting method or the monitoring range. The use of multiple fixed cameras will enable the security surveillance center to pick up detailed images from a wide area. Also, the use of PTZ cameras can aid in obtaining detailed images.

The following factors should be taken into consideration when conducting an overview of the environment that the security surveillance center cameras, and equipment are planned to be installed or located.

Temperature

The average operating temperature range for cameras in general is between 14°F and 122°F. Always confirm operating temperature ranges with manufacturer specifications to ensure that the cameras are designed to operate normally in your climate. If the environment that the cameras will be located is outside of the operating temperature range, there are options available that will help them to endure higher or lower temperatures. For environments that have higher temperatures than are recommended for the camera to perform at its optimum level, protective camera housings can be outfitted with coolers or fans that keep the camera cool so that it can perform properly. For environments that have lower temperatures than are recommended for the camera to perform at its optimum level, protective camera housings can be outfitted with heaters or other devices that keep the camera warm so that it can perform properly.

Humidity

If humidity gets inside of a camera or lens, it can be one of the worst things that could happen to the equipment because it can lead to the rusting and corrosion of the metal parts of the equipment. This can result in the life of the equipment being shortened due to the corrosion and rusting of the metallic parts. One way to identify if humidity or condensation is developing is the formation of water droplets on a solid surface. To prevent this moisture from entering the camera, it is highly recommended that the camera be housed within a sealed case.

Rain and Dust

Whenever security surveillance center cameras or equipment are located in areas where they could be exposed to elements such as water or dust, they should be placed in protective housings. For example, waterproof or water-resistant housings should be used wherever cameras or equipment have the possibility of being exposed to rain, water, or any type of precipitation or droplets of water. Also, in areas where the possibility exists that cameras or equipment may be exposed to dust, housings that provide protection from dust should be used to protect the cameras and equipment. Depending on ambient temperature and humidity, the front glass panel of the camera casing may become clouded by condensation or frost.

Lens Selection

Two of the key factors to consider when making a lens selection are: the location or position of the camera and the desired coverage area to be captured on the camera image. Remember the following when choosing between a wide-angle or narrow-angle lens:

- Wide-angle lenses provide wide coverage of an area, and images, such as people, will appear smaller.
- The wider the coverage area, the smaller the images will appear. Conversely, the narrower the camera coverage, the larger a subject or object will appear.
- Wide-angle lenses help to eliminate blind spots within a room, because they cover a larger or wider area.
- When monitoring an entire room, a wide-angle lens should be used.

CAMERA SIGNAL TO MONITOR OR SCREEN

When selecting the monitors or screens, the size of the security surveillance center, the monitor/screen display method, the number of monitors/screens, and the number of areas to be monitored are key factors that need to be determined prior to the installation and setup of any security surveillance center.

There are many different configurations that can be utilized when the signal is routed from a camera to the recorder, screen, or monitor. The best analogy I can think of to describe the way a signal goes from the camera to the recorder, screen, or monitor is to compare it to an old-fashioned phone switchboard, where a phone call is received by an operator and the call is then assigned to a specific device or phone. In the case of the security surveillance center system, the signal is sent out from the camera and is received by a hardware device, or a set of hardware devices, commonly referred to as a switch. The "switch" then takes the input from the camera signal and joins it with the remote controls for the camera. The signal is then assigned to the outputs (i.e., the recorder, screen, or monitor). Another type of "switch" is known as a virtual switch that can be found in newer security surveillance systems. With this type of system, cameras go into the computer and the software assigns the cameras to monitors, screens, and recorders. This type of setup also addresses remote controls. The switch allows the system to have more than one remote controller. For example, the security surveillance center will have one, and the general manager may want to have one of his or her own. Regardless of how many switches are provided, the security surveillance center must have the ability to override all others in the event of an emergency or urgent investigation.

RECORDERS

Gone are the days of video cassette recorders (VCRs). I can remember when every video cassette had to be replaced in every VCR every 8 hours. This resulted in three tapes per day being stored for at least 2 weeks. Do the math—that is a lot of VCR tapes that had to be stored and rotated each week. Besides the storage space needed to keep the VCR tapes for at least two, other challenges that were encountered included the following:

- VCR tape quality or the tape breaking during a review.
  - If all the VCR tapes were not replaced on a predetermined schedule, poor quality of playback and tape breakage could occur.
- When a VCR tape was removed for review it needed to be immediately replaced.
  - If this did not occur and a review of an area that was supposed to be covered by the tape removed, there would not be any coverage to review.

With today's modern systems, the DVR is much better for many reasons, including it is easier to use, quality of playback is reliable, and longer time periods can be stored than with physical storage of tapes. DVRs play a key role in the process of any security surveillance center and the camera connection to a monitor or screen. A DVR is a multichannel analog input device that captures composite video, stores it on digital media, and enables security surveillance center personnel to search, playback, and perform video analysis functions on a monitor or screen. The following steps are taken for the security surveillance center to get real-time and recorded video from a laptop, mobile device, desktop computer, and other devices, via a browser: The camera should be connected to a portal, network switch, or Wi-Fi router, and the camera identification information should be programmed at the security surveillance center. When selecting the video recorder configuration, it is important to remember that the higher the frame rate, the smoother the playback. However, the trade-off is that it will require more storage space. When selecting the frame rate, a view of a stationary object can have a lower frame rate, whereas the frame rate of a person at a POS at a cash register should be higher so that all parts of a transaction are viewable and the exchange of money and product is observed and identifiable. Also, remember that the following will increase storage limits:

- When the recorded camera resolution is increased, it will increase the storage limits proportionally.
- PTZ cameras and panning cameras use more storage than fixed cameras that have little activity. This is due to compression, not frame rate.

Network video recorders (NVR) are digital but may be computer or server based. NVR records as a DVR and stores data on servers that are linked. When a server is full, it switches to one that is not. One or more servers are able to be used as backup servers, and they can store data or begin storing data when another server fails.

A best practice is to implement a replacement schedule for the equipment utilized in the security surveillance center. This information is useful for budgeting purposes, especially during the annual capital expenditures projects request for additional funding. A detailed list of all the equipment should include the following information:

- Make
- Model
- Serial number
- Supplier
- Location installed
- Date purchased
- Purchase price
- Projected replacement date—this can be based on the manufacturer's antic-ipated life cycle of the equipment.

In addition to a replacement schedule, schematic drawings of the security surveillance system should be made. Anytime any changes are made to the security surveillance system, the schematic drawings must be updated and should be reviewed on a consistent basis. The schematic drawings should include the following:

- All camera locations
  - Type of camera (PTZ, fixed, etc.)
  - Direction camera is pointing in the "at rest" position
  - Projected replacement date
- All equipment locations
  - Type of equipment
  - Wiring/power specifications

MONITORS AND SCREENS

The security surveillance console should be designed so that the interface between the equipment and operator is ergonomically balanced and easy to use. The human engineering aspect (ergonomics) should be carefully considered in the selection and design of the security surveillance center. Some factors to consider are lighting, noise, room temperature, graphic displays, and general comfort factors. These elements provide an environment that enhances the security surveillance center operator's effectiveness and reduces frustration and fatigue. High temperatures and uncomfortable chairs can cause fatigue, and background noises distract the operator, which can lead to lowered performance. Conversely, adjustable lighting levels allow illumination to be chosen as desired for enhancement of the viewing contrast on the security surveillance monitor displays.

Well-designed graphical user interfaces (GUIs) provide a capability for enhanced display of security alarm information in computer-based systems. A good design limits the ways information is displayed and places constraints on which operations are permitted. A good menu should not have more than nine items and should not be nestled more than three levels.

Another area of importance is the use of color on maps, menus, buttons, and backgrounds. Although color can be an effective aid in highlighting important information, it should be used sparingly. Keep in mind that about 10% of the population has some form of color blindness, therefore security surveillance centers should not be solely dependent on colors to operate a system. If colors are used they should be kept to seven or fewer. Every time a color is added to a screen, it adds to the perceived complexity of the display. Remember consistent shades of colors should be used, with gray being a common color choice, and primary colors should be used to indicate sensor status. For example,

- Red for alarms
- Yellow for access
- Green for secure status

Console selection is one of the most important aspects of the design. At first glance, it looks like an easy choice of simply placing a counter in the room, but a closer look reveals that there are many decisions that need to be made regarding this fundamental piece of equipment. Some elements to consider when reviewing the various products during the selection include how the counter will be used and what items will be on the console counter:

- Use of the computer and keyboard
- Answering telephones
- Taking phone messages
- Writing reports
- Taking notes
- Issuing identification badges
- Performing duties that involve writing or typing
- Viewing CCTV monitors on the console counter

A major component of the security surveillance center involves video surveillance. Depending on the property, the number of cameras viewed by the security surveillance operator will vary depending on the industry, the environment, and the philosophy of the company. Video coverage may vary significantly, ranging from a few cameras to hundreds or even thousands. It is important to note that the maximum number of displays that one security surveillance operator should view is 16, and this includes alarms.

An important area of concern in the security surveillance center is the location where any images are printed, video copies are generated, or materials and information are distributed. Checks and balances should be implemented to mitigate the risks involved. One key component of due diligence in protecting this area is the installation of camera coverage of any area where images are printed, video copies are generated, or materials and information are distributed. These cameras are also useful tracking tools to clarify any questions or concerns that might arise, such as

- Who visited this sensitive area?
- Who was issued information?
- What department was issued information?

- Were processes followed?
- Were checks and balances practiced?
- Were standard operating procedures followed?

The security surveillance center should be operator-friendly. Control panels should be straightforward and simple, while monitors should be easy to view. Help and instruction displays should be designed in a manner to provide assistance in a way that an operator can quickly and efficiently access and cope with serious situations. Instructions should be written and communicated in a simple, plain, and easily understood manner. Security surveillance center personnel often work under stressful conditions, and integrating these elements into the design of the security surveillance center greatly improves the ability of the personnel to efficiently and effectively receive information, dispatch personnel, and obtain a positive resolution to any incident, emergency, or crisis.

When determining the placement of monitors or screens into the security surveillance center, it is important to take into consideration the width of the room and ceiling height. The distance of the security surveillance center wall from personnel who are operating and viewing the CCTV monitors depends on the width of the wall. If the wall is narrow, then the distance needs to be closer; if the wall is wide, then it needs to be further back. In other words, if there are security surveillance monitors or screens spread across the wall, the security surveillance center personnel will need to be farther from the security surveillance wall to be able to view all of the monitors or screens more easily. It is important to keep the proper distance so that a lot of head movement is not necessary—ideally, personnel should only have to move their eyes side to side to see the entire security surveillance wall.

The recommended optimum distance of security surveillance center personnel from the monitor depends on the size of the screen or monitor. The following are recommended maximum and minimum viewing distances based on the size of the security surveillance screens or monitors. For example, if security surveillance center personnel are viewing a 12-inch monitor—measured diagonally—the viewing range should be a minimum of 24 inches and a maximum of 60 inches. Generally, through my experiences in setting up security surveillance centers, I have found that the general viewing distances should range between two and five times the size of the monitor—measured diagonally.

For example, if six 42-inch monitors are placed on the wall, the ceiling height should be at least 8 feet high. Also, enough space should be provided so that the workstations are at least 7 feet and as far as 17.5 feet from the wall. This combined with the lighting being dimmed should enable the security surveillance center personnel to concentrate on the monitors and provide them with a comfortable view. Methods that should be used to reduce eye fatigue of security surveillance center personnel include the following:

- Overhead lights and lights behind or to the side of the monitor should not be mounted in a way that would reflect off of the front surface of the monitor.
- Glare-reducing screen or monitor overlays should be used.
- The face of the screen or monitor should be in the direction of a darkened area of the room.

Unfortunately, sometimes the space and location provided for the security surveillance center may be factors in determining the viewing distance. If this should be the case, always attempt to situate the security surveillance center personnel viewing the security surveillance wall within the recommended ranges. When a security surveillance center has dimensions that are not ideal, it may call for a creative solution in order to maximize the viewing distance. One example is that it may require the setup of the security surveillance wall in one corner, and the security surveillance center personnel may have their workstations set up diagonally in the opposite corner viewing the security surveillance wall.

Another important concern when setting up the security surveillance center is limiting eye fatigue by controlling the angles and viewing distances that security surveillance center personnel may experience while viewing monitors. The recommended maximum horizontal viewing angle in both directions is approximately 45°. The maximum vertical viewing angle between observer line of sight and the monitor for acceptable monitor image distortion is approximately 30°. Security surveillance center monitors or screens on the video wall in areas that have less activity should be placed on the outer edges of the wall and should be smaller in size. These monitors or screens are utilized to detect movement, not detail. For example, the views could include a safe, employee parking lot at night when the property is closed, and so on. Larger monitors or screens should be placed near the center of the video wall at eye level. These should be views of important areas of activity such as retail areas, main entrance areas, and so forth. There should be two or three monitors located on the workstations directly in front of the security surveillance center operators. These should be used to show alarms, patrols, etc.

The monitors utilized by security surveillance center personnel should have the monitor screen at a distance of at least 20 inches away. Having the monitor screen at a relatively long viewing distance allows the users' eyes to relax. A general rule of thumb is that security surveillance center personnel should have the monitor screen at least one full arm's length away from their eyes while seated. Security surveillance center personnel should also adjust monitor screens to a viewing angle of around 15° lower than the horizontal level. This viewing angle will reduce visual discomfort, such as dry eyes, and musculoskeletal discomfort, such as neck and back pain. Also, security surveillance center personnel should follow the 20/20/20 rule recommended by clinical optometrists. After 20 minutes of computer use, security surveillance center personnel should look at something 20 feet away for at least 20 seconds.

The three primary classifications of video surveillance systems are observation, review, and recognition. The resolution for observation does not have as high resolution requirements as recognition but requires high frame (refresh) rates. Systems used primarily for review after an incident occurs should have excellent coverage and a frame rate high enough to capture an event.

Recognition types of systems that analyze video, like license plate recognition, require the highest resolution or amount of pixels. At a very large casino I opened, one of these systems was installed at the entrance of a parking garage and it was quite useful on several levels. For example, we were able to create a database that associated license plates with people. This was useful in that we could determine if a person associated with a vehicle was in our parking garage and possibly on the property. This system was used to aid law enforcement, the marketing team, and many others. To deploy systems like these and conserve storage or bandwidth, a trigger should be provided to activate the recognition-based recording and a vehicle loop detector should be used to activate a camera that performs a license plate recognition function.

Another key component that impacts the effectiveness of a security surveillance system is lighting levels. The proper lighting levels are important for monitoring activities on the security surveillance system. Other benefits are that they deter crime, displace unwanted activity, and provide a sense of safety and security. The American Institute of Architects recommends the following minimum lighting levels measured in foot candles (fc). A foot candle is a unit of illumination—it is equal to that given by a light source. It is equal to 1 candela at a distance of 1 foot—equal to 1 lumen per square foot:

- Landscape—0.5 fc
- Roadways—0.5 fc
- Areas close to building—1 fc
- Walkways—1.5 fc
- Building entrances—5 fc
- Parking garages—5 fc
- Parking lots—5 fc

Keep in mind that the lighting requirements for security surveillance center monitoring generally require at least 1 to 2 fc of illumination. The lighting recommended for areas involving life and safety considerations in garages, parking lots, and other external locations is at least 5 fc and higher.

In areas where artificial lighting is not preferred, infrared cameras can be used. This enables the area to be monitored by the security surveillance center without the need for additional artificial lighting. This is extremely effective in areas that have low lighting. This enables surveillance of an area without the use of additional visible lighting. Since this does not require additional lighting, it does not alert those who enter the view of the cameras and makes this application useful for convert surveillance. This is extremely effective in low-light areas and can provide security surveillance center personnel the ability to see in the dark.

The security surveillance center is generally responsible for the access control of a property. The role of security surveillance personnel in regard to access control is to ensure that visitors, personnel, and material are only permitted access to areas in which they are authorized to enter, and only authorized material is permitted to be removed from the property.

Visitors, vendors, and contractors should sign in and sign out at the security surveillance center upon entering and exiting the property. The sign-in and sign-out log should include the following information:

- Name
- Date
- Signature

- Who is being visited
- Arrival time
- Departure time
- Contact telephone number (in case of emergency)
- Security surveillance center personnel name
- Security surveillance center personnel signature

Upon arrival, the visitor, vendor, or contractor should present a state or federal photo identification such as a driver's license to security surveillance center personnel. Once the information is obtained and verified, a badge is issued and displayed and is to be worn at all times. The badge is not to leave the property. If the visitor, vendor, or contractor departs the property, the badge must be returned and signed back in at the security surveillance center and the log is completed including the departure time.

Generally, the security surveillance center should be designed with ergonomic considerations. Ergonomics takes into consideration general comfort factors that provide a security surveillance center environment that enhances the personnel's effectiveness and reduces frustration and fatigue. The layout of the security surveillance center is a key factor in how effectively and efficiently the area will run. A well-designed security surveillance center can increase the physical comfort, reduce stress levels, and improve efficiencies of the demanding role and the tasks that security surveillance center personnel perform. The security surveillance center console should be designed so that the interface between the equipment and operator is ergonomically balanced and easy to use. The human engineering aspect (ergonomics) should be carefully considered in the selection and design of the security surveillance center.

Some factors to consider are lighting, noise, room temperature, graphic displays, and general comfort factors. These elements provide an environment that enhances the security surveillance center operator's effectiveness and reduces frustration and fatigue. High temperatures and uncomfortable chairs can cause fatigue, and background noises distract the operator and can lead to lower performance. Conversely, adjustable lighting levels allow illumination to be chosen as desired for enhancement of the viewing contrast on the security surveillance monitor displays. The physical layout and the ergonomics of the security surveillance center workstations should be considered in their totality. The equipment should have the ability to be adjusted so that security surveillance center personnel have the ability to make adjustments, which make it possible to assume the proper posture while making it the most comfortable for personnel.

The level of mental workload experienced by operators is a key element in the effectiveness, reliability, and efficiency of security surveillance centers. Workload can be described as the security surveillance center personnel's ability to be attentive while performing security surveillance center tasks. The level of mental workload represents the proportion of resources that are required to meet the task demands.

It is important to determine the proper workload for security surveillance center personnel. When security surveillance center personnel are faced with excessive tasks and their attentional resources are exceeded, they become overloaded and are prone to errors. Mental overload of security surveillance center personnel occurs when the demands of tasks are so great that they become detrimental to their performance. The opposite is also true: when security surveillance center personnel experience excessively low task demands, they may experience a state of mental underload that can also be detrimental to their performance. Since each person is unique, the monitoring of performance, ability, and aptitude should occur on a regular basis, and determinations should be made in regard to the workload range or the work zone each can perform while being not being excessively overloaded or excessively underloaded. This will result in the security surveillance center and its personnel performing at maximum effectiveness and efficiency.

There are various consequences associated with inappropriate levels of workload, which can lead to the following performance decrements:

- Inattention
- Complacency
- Fatigue
- Monotony
- Reduced vigilance
- Stress

In conclusion of this chapter, I would like you to keep the following in mind. Security surveillance center personnel are your most valuable asset. Security surveillance center designs and equipment can be changed and replaced without having an impact on the dynamics of the department and the esprit de corps of the team. The way the team interacts, supports, and energizes one another will be a major factor in establishing, and sustaining, a great security surveillance center. The most important elements in ensuring the successful operation of any security surveillance center are selecting the best-qualified candidates, providing training, providing the tools and equipment needed to perform their duties, developing a sense of trust among the team, and performing the basics with brilliance.

3 Security Surveillance Center Processes

The following should provide security surveillance center personnel with the processes to utilize the security surveillance center to its fullest extent and capability. These processes and best practices should provide maximum protection, identification, and detection of any activity or crisis that could impact the property. Implementation of these processes and best practices should enable the security surveillance center to provide a safe and secure environment. The proper processes and best practices should also allow the security surveillance center to produce usable video to determine the sequence of events of an incident and the visual facts as they relate to any situation. The following are some basic processes and best practices that should be adhered to in any security surveillance center.

- Staff the security surveillance center 24 hours a day, 7 days a week, 365 days a year.
- Have at least one member of the security surveillance center team on duty at all times.
- Leave cameras in their "at rest" positions when not in use. When possible, design these positions to provide the ability to locate and track a subject anywhere on the property. If funds are not available, plan forward to make this possible in the future.
- Monitor individuals who loiter in areas. They may be setting up for a theft or other activity.
- Provide security surveillance center personnel with training and techniques to increase their understanding of detection of theft, recognize safety hazards, and address other identified areas of concern.
- Provide security surveillance center operators with techniques to properly gather video evidence and information.
- Ensure proper setup and display of monitors and cameras so that security surveillance center operators are able to use them proactively and effectively.
- Ensure that setup and display are dictated by property needs, past experiences, types of incidents, and event types.
- Establish coverage at the entrances, exits, back of house, and high traffic/event areas for the protection of internal and external customers.
- Ensure effective setup of the security surveillance center system to provide operators with the ability to conduct proactive operations, provide timely response with minimal effort, identify suspects, and provide information for effective investigations.

- Investigate all violations of policy and procedure. Violations can be indicative of theft or other prohibited acts.
- Do not permit beverages on the console. If beverages are permitted in the security surveillance center, they should have covers on the containers.
- Do not permit personal phone calls from the security surveillance center.
- Clean the security surveillance center before the end of every shift.
- Complete and review for accuracy all paperwork prior to the completion of the security surveillance center operators' shift.
- Ensure that briefing and information are exchanged between security surveillance center personnel at the start of the shift and when relieved.
- After equipment checklist is completed, immediately report any issues to a member of the security surveillance center leadership team.
- Ensure pertinent information is accurate and up to date.
- Answer the telephone within three rings.
  - The proper way to answer the telephone is as follows: "Good Morning/ Good Afternoon/Good Evening. Security Surveillance Center, [*your first name*], speaking. How may I assist you?"
  - Note the time the call came in, the person's name, the issue, and the location.
  - Make appropriate notifications and notify a member of the security surveillance center leadership team if warranted.
  - If a call back to the initial caller is necessary, be sure to correctly record the name and phone number of the caller.
- Monitor and complete closed-circuit television (CCTV) camera checks.
- Dispatch personnel as needed.
- Maintain and document information.
- Issue temporary credentials to employees, visitors, and vendors.
- Ensure that the security surveillance center is the checkpoint for the inspection of package passes and ensuring persons leaving the property are not in possession of any unauthorized items. The basic rule of thumb is that if someone did not bring an item onto the property, then that person must have a package pass to leave with it.
- Ensure communication and notification between departments and outside agencies (i.e., fire, police, etc.).
- Monitor and control access to restricted access doors.
- Monitor and acknowledge the alarm system. Dispatch personnel to the alarm location.
- Contact the Incident Command Center for emergency incidents.
- Ensure that all equipment (i.e., phones, computer, radio, etc.) is operational. Damaged or problematic equipment or systems should be reported immediately to a member of the security surveillance center leadership team.
- Make emergency notifications for the following incidents:
  - Biological, chemical, suspicious substance incidents
  - Bomb threats, evacuations, general (priority 1) fire alarm
  - Critical medical response incidents, including first aid, CPR, AED events
  - Labor actions, strikes, pickets, demonstrations, and work interruptions

- Major crimes including armed robberies, strong arm robberies, aggravated assaults, crime with weapons, crimes where persons (patron or employee) are injured
- Police or fire personnel on site responding to an incident, such as
  - Serious danger or hazardous conditions, severe property damage or flooding
  - Sudden deaths, suicide, homicide, hostage, jumper incident, patron or employee serious injury
  - Terror threats, change in terror threat level, or homeland security incident

When in doubt, contact a member of the security surveillance center leadership team.

CCTV FAILURE

The security surveillance center contingency process for a CCTV camera outage is designed to provide a coordinated course of action in the event that the ability of the security surveillance center CCTV camera system goes out of service. In the event that the property loses camera capabilities during a power outage, or for any other reason, the following measures will be taken to ensure the integrity of the security surveillance center:

- If the system fails, all efforts will be made to maintain the confidentiality of the knowledge of the failure. The security surveillance center leader will immediately be notified.
- The information will be disseminated on a need-to-know basis to the leaders in key and critical areas. After an assessment of the failure, the leadership team of the security surveillance center will determine the estimated time it will take to bring the system back online.

In the event that the property loses camera capabilities during a power outage, or for any other reason, the following measures will be taken to ensure the integrity of the security surveillance center:

- Security surveillance center personnel may be recalled in plain clothes to provide security surveillance of key areas of the property, including, but not limited to, the monitoring of money handling areas.
- Security surveillance center personnel will have specific job duties and responsibilities.

In the event that a commercial power failure occurs, the emergency generators are designed to automatically switch on. These generators are designed to accommodate predesignated emergency systems including the following:

Security surveillance center
Life safety equipment

Emergency lighting
Passenger elevators
Exit stairways
Telephone equipment
Smoke exhaust fans
Computer equipment

ALARMS

When a general fire alarm is received and an emergency has been determined, the security surveillance center should notify the local fire department to respond. When an alarm is transmitted and received at the security surveillance center, the operator should immediately notify the appropriate departments of the alarm. The security surveillance center should contact the highest-ranking security surveillance center representative and provide an update of the situation. The security surveillance center should dispatch personnel to the fire command center to provide an escort for the responding fire department. Responding departments, other than the security surveillance center personnel, will dispatch appropriate personnel to the alarm location. Ensure that the security surveillance center personnel remain at their positions throughout a fire emergency, unless their lives are endangered or they are directed to vacate their positions. No information concerning a fire or emergency should be given to the media or bystanders. All such requests should be referred to the proper representative or designee of the property.

When representatives arrive on location, a report of the status of the situation should be communicated by radio or phone to the security surveillance center, giving all conditions of the alarm area. On all priority and general alarms that have been investigated longer than 3 minutes, the security surveillance center should notify the local fire department. In the event of an actual fire, the security surveillance center should coordinate the following:

- Assign personnel to await the arrival of the fire department.
- Hand out communication devices to the fire department.
- Upon the arrival of the fire department, assign personnel to escort them to the emergency scene or location. The representative on the scene will report all conditions as they pertain to the emergency.

If deemed necessary and the emergency warrants it, the security surveillance center may serve as a "command post." This location should be equipped with a telephone, table, and chairs. The use of all equipment—radios, telephone, CCTV, and so on—should be maintained and controlled from this area.

LIFE SAFETY/FIRE COMMAND

The following is generally the process and procedures for various jurisdictions. For the specific requirements in your areas of responsibility, please consult with and refer to your local jurisdictional representatives.

SENSOR SELECTION

The following factors should be considered when choosing fire sensors:

- *State and local codes*: Verify that sensors meet all applicable code requirements including the requirements of the Underwriters Laboratories, NFPA Codes, and National Electrical Manufacturers Association.
- *Local authorities*: Local fire authorities should be consulted during the planning stages to ensure that sensors conform to applicable codes, advice on best practices, and evacuation plans.
- *Type of occupancy*: The following characteristics should be taken into consideration: types of materials stored, processed, and human factors when selecting detection devices.
- *Physical considerations*: Size, layout, and interior configuration should be taken into consideration when selecting sensor types.
- *Number of buildings*: Larger structures and complexes may use a variety of technologies. Ensure that all systems and sensors have the ability to work well together.

STAGES OF FIRE

It is important that the security surveillance center operator be familiar with the fire triangle (Figure 3.1), the elements of the progression of fire, and the repercussions of each stage. The following are the four stages of fire:

- *Incipient stage*: Invisible products of combustion are generated with no visible smoke or appreciable heat.
- *Smoldering stage*: Smoke is visible without the presence of flame or appreciable heat.
- *Flammable stage*: Flames or fire exist. Although appreciable heat is not present, it usually follows instantaneously.
- *Heat stage*: Uncontrolled heat and rapidly expanding air are present.

EVACUATIONS

Any general alarm causes a property to evacuate automatically. Evacuations should be made on the basis of activation of initiating devices and/or confirmation from a reliable source of fire via phone and/or radio. Certain situations may dictate an investigative phase before an evacuation occurs. Once an evacuation begins, there should not be any consultation with any party in regard to the halting of an evacuation.

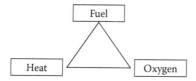

FIGURE 3.1   The fire triangle. Elements needed for a fire to ignite.

The only deviation from this is that the fire department may order, alter, or halt any evacuation once they take control of the facility. In the event of a property evacuation, all employees will direct patrons to exit the building.

ANNOUNCEMENT OF EVACUATION

The order to evacuate should be conducted using the manual public address system, and the message should be prewritten in terms that are simple, explicit, brief, and to the point. It should state what area or areas are being evacuated, where the people are to go, and how they are to get there. Inflammatory words or phrases are to be avoided. For example, the word "bomb" should never be used. The ethnic makeup of the population being addressed should be considered. If feasible, it should be broadcast in English, Spanish, and possibly other languages if particular foreign language-speaking groups are known to be present.

The following is an example of an evacuation message: "May we have your attention please. There has been an emergency reported in the building. Please proceed calmly to the nearest emergency exit. Thank you." Repeat the message accordingly. The announcement should be made clearly and calmly in a controlled voice to direct and inform while not unnecessarily exciting guests or employees. Once the order to evacuate is given, it is to be carried out without delay in a calm and professional manner.

Communications

Priority for incoming calls should be in the following order:

1. Fire department/police department/emergency services
2. Security surveillance center locations
3. Extensions in affected or involved areas
4. In-house phones
5. Outside calls

EVACUATION PROCEDURES

In any evacuation occurrence, the security surveillance center will have primary responsibility for assuring the evacuation of public areas, and the evacuation should be carried out in the manner prescribed and to the extent ordered. Other employees and available resources may be utilized to assist. Security surveillance center personnel will be responsible for ensuring that the evacuated rooms or areas are secured following the evacuation. They may only be reoccupied when the proper authorities give permission to do so. It is important that all related activities be communicated to the security surveillance center. In implementing the evacuation, the following processes should be adhered to by security surveillance center personnel:

- The safety of guests and employees should always be the first consideration and priority.

- Protection and safeguarding of assets, both of guests and the company, should be the second priority.
- Review of key areas with the CCTV system should occur to ensure the evacuation processes are completed.

The highest-ranking member of the security surveillance center leadership team should be the person in charge of the security surveillance center during the crisis. Upon receiving instructions to evacuate the property or any part thereof, or having reason to believe that the evacuation will or may occur, the following steps should be taken:

- A member of the security surveillance center team should make all necessary telephone notifications, including calling in additional security surveillance center personnel if it is anticipated that they may be needed.
- Inform representatives of the security surveillance center leadership team of the situation, explaining it as fully as possible.
- A security surveillance center representative should be assigned to investigate any reported injuries or claims that are immediately reported as a result of the evacuation.
- The security surveillance center should be made aware of any event at the time of the event. Review of coverage should be conducted and reported back to the personnel handling the incident.
- Make arrangements to procure necessary keys permitting entry to employee offices or other locations that are anticipated to be evacuated.
- Assign a security surveillance center representative to keep a detailed log of people removed from the premises for treatment.

PROPERTY EVACUATIONS

No information concerning a fire or emergency should be given to the media or bystanders. All such requests should be referred to personnel responsible for this area or the designee. Elevators should not be used in the event of a fire. As elevator shafts are similar to chimneys, smoke and toxic gases can enter the elevator shaft and asphyxiate the occupants. Internal and external guests should use the fire exits during an emergency fire situation.

Should it become necessary to evacuate the property, time permitting, the security surveillance center should coordinate the assembly of the highest-ranking member of the security surveillance center leadership team and explain the situation as it is known. Specific assignments and responsibilities should be issued accordingly. The responsibilities should include assuring that key and critical areas are secured prior to, during, and following the evacuation and that areas are properly and totally evacuated. Once the evacuation announcement is made over the public address system, all available personnel should assist and direct patrons in leaving the property via the nearest emergency exit, as long as it is safe to do so. All exit doors should be secured in the open position until the property is cleared. Personnel should be assigned to the entrances/exits and should remain there until further notice to assist patrons out and not permit reentry back into the property until authorized by the fire department.

General Information

- If necessary, handicapped guests should be escorted.
- Speak politely to all guests, but insist on complete compliance.
- A professional and calm demeanor exhibited by employees during an emergency evacuation plays a key role in the safe evacuation of any facility. Remain calm and professional during all interactions.
- Anyone who has been evacuated is not to be allowed reentry, until the facility is deemed safe and the *all clear* announcement is given.
- All employees should familiarize themselves with all regular and emergency exits.
- All property personnel should report to predetermined locations, on the outside of the facility. A head count and roll call should be taken, and if any employees are not accounted for, the security surveillance center should be notified immediately.
- It is of the utmost importance that when evacuation procedures are in progress, evacuees cannot be permitted to cluster around the immediate exterior of the building.

All department leaders should ensure that their team is aware of the following:

1. Locations of fire emergency exit doors in their work area
2. Locations and how to operate fire extinguishers
3. The primary evacuation meeting place located outside the complex

EMERGENCY EQUIPMENT—INVENTORY AND INSPECTION

Emergency equipment including rope, bullhorns, fire blankets, flashlights, first aid kits, clipboards, pencils, and markers should be stored in the security surveillance center. These articles are to be available to personnel, or others, should they be required during an emergency. Representatives of the security surveillance center leadership team should periodically inspect the emergency equipment to make sure that it is in good working order and to maintain an inventory reflective of the needs of the property.

TIME SYNCHRONIZATION

An area that is often overlooked is the synchronization of time stamps of the different types of systems utilized in an organization. The importance of all systems operating on the same time and having the same time stamp is crucial when reports of various systems are gathered for investigations, court appearances or legal presentations. All systems that have a time stamp like a time clock, report writing systems, access control systems, video systems, and so on, should be synchronized on Network Time Protocol (NTP). The synchronization of time should be in the same time zone of the property, and atomic time is a good resource to use to set this standard. NTP should also be on a wall clock in the security surveillance center so that all operators can refer to it when completing logs, information tracking forms and to make sure the time is accurate on the various systems.

BADGES

There are various types of badges that the security surveillance center is responsible for. These temporary badges include construction site access badges, employee badges, vendor badges, and visitor badges. The following are examples of how each can be addressed in a systematic manner that will account for the life cycle of a property badge.

In my career, I have been involved in many openings of properties including the opening of various casinos, restaurants, retail stores, arenas, hotels, entertainment complexes, and night clubs all across the United States. The following are guidelines, processes, and recommendations that should be included pertaining to the badging process for the construction of a new property or the expansion of a new section of a property.

CONTRACTORS

The following are guidelines for construction site security surveillance center access badges for contractors and visitors:

- There should be one location for issuance and return of contractor and visitor badges. This location should be the security surveillance center.
- The security surveillance center should issue and control all contractor and visitor badges.
- The security surveillance center should systematically record and track the issuance, return, and destruction of all issued badges.
- Final payments to contractors should be held until the issued badges are accounted for.
- In the event that a new contractor identification badge system is implemented—and as of a predetermined date—all previously issued contractor identification cards should no longer be valid.
- The contractor badges should limit the contractor(s) to a specific area or level. Contractors should only be granted permission to the level or area in which they are contracted to work. Contractors should not be granted badges that provide access to the entire project. If a contractor is observed and reported to be in an unauthorized area, the contractor may be banned from the property.
- The types of badges issued should emphasize simplicity, consistency and be easily identifiable.
- A badge checking system should be implemented with established monitored checkpoints which includes the main entrance and elevators.

Construction Site Visitor Badges

The purpose of the construction site visitor badge is to verify and control the access of visitors to this area. Construction site visitors' badges must be displayed at all times and are available at the security surveillance center. Security surveillance center personnel will record the following information on the construction site visitor badge log:

- Date
- Employee number
- Visitor's name
- Authorized by
- Time issued
- Area to visit
- Security surveillance center representative signature and identification number
- The badge should then be assigned a control number and issued to the visitor
- While on tour, the visitor should be accompanied by a representative authorized to be in the areas visited
- There should be one location for issuance and return of visitor badges
- Visitors should be required to leave a photo ID—including driver's license, employee ID, and so on—when issued a visitor badge
- The color of the visitor badges should be changed to a different color every day. Anyone displaying the improper color should immediately be reported to the security surveillance center
- Visitor badges are considered day passes and need to be renewed on a daily basis
- Visitors should not be permitted to take photographs unless permission is received in advance from the project/property leader
- When the issued visitor badge is returned, the photo ID will be returned to the visitor
- Visitors should be required to sign a release and waiver form

During the construction phases of a new property, or the addition to an existing property, a variety of people representing various organizations visit the construction site. Many are excited to have the opportunity to see the latest and greatest, with safety being one of the last things on their mind. The following is a sample of a construction site access release and waiver of liability. This advises all visitors of the possible dangers that one may be exposed to, and the expected behavior of visitors to the construction site.

CONSTRUCTION SITE ACCESS RELEASE
FORM AND WAIVER OF LIABILITY

In consideration of being granted the right to visit the construction site for the NAME OF PROPERTY located at PROJECT SITE, being constructed by NAME OF COMPANY, I acknowledge, agree, and represent that I am aware that the Project Site is under construction and that a construction site is a dangerous environment, despite the precautions for safety taken by PROPERTY NAME, its general contractor, and other trade contractors performing work at the project site. I agree:

1. To the fullest extent permitted by law, I hereby release, waive, discharge, and covenant not to sue NAME OF COMPANY or any of its respective parents, affiliates, members, or subsidiaries and its individual officers, shareholders, employees, and agents (the "Releasees"), from any and all liability, arising from my negligence or otherwise, as a result of my participation in the site tour, including, but not limited to, liability for property damage or loss, or bodily, personal, or mental injury, including death.
2. I further agree to hold harmless and indemnify the "Releasees" against any liability arising from my negligence or otherwise and from damages of any kind as a result of my participation in the site tour.
3. I acknowledge that it is my sole responsibility to evaluate carefully the risks inherent in visiting the PROJECT SITE and that I have fully considered those risks, including, without limitation, dangers posed by willful or negligent conduct of myself and/or by others. I also understand that I will wear appropriate personal protection to include, but not be limited to, hard hat, eye protection, reflective safety vest, and proper work boots.
4. I acknowledge and voluntarily assume full responsibility for, and full risk of, property damage or loss, or bodily, mental, or personal injury, including death, relating to my participation in the site tour.
5. I acknowledge that I am not an employee of "Releasees" during participation in the visit to the PROJECT SITE.
6. I understand that no photographs are permitted to be taken of the PROJECT SITE or any part thereof during the site tour and that no materials or products may be removed from the PROJECT SITE.
7. I agree that if any portion of this document is held invalid, the remaining provisions shall be binding and continue in full force and effect.

I have read the Visitor Release Form and Waiver of Liability carefully, understand its significance, and voluntarily agree to all of its terms.

Visitor (print name) _____ Signature Date _____

Visitor Signature _____ Emergency Phone # _____

Name of Emergency Contact _____ Relationship _____

NOTE: All required signatures must be completed and this form returned before the visitor may visit the project site.

BADGES—TEMPORARY BADGES FOR EMPLOYEES

Security surveillance center personnel will be equipped to issue temporary badge credentials to employees. Security surveillance center personnel will provide the employee with a temporary badge only after they

- Verify the employee is listed as an active employee.
- Confirm information with employee's supervisor.

BADGES—TEMPORARY BADGES FOR VENDORS

Security surveillance center personnel will be equipped to issue temporary badge credentials to vendors. The security surveillance center will be notified of the presence of the vendor employee but will not need to physically have personnel accompany the employee if the leader in charge of the area agrees to the unescorted presence of the vendor employee.

The vendor employee will be required to sign in at the security surveillance center, where the vendor employee's name, company, vendor ID number, and the department in which he or she will be working will be logged in.

The security surveillance center will issue the vendor employee a vendor badge that must be worn the entire time the vendor employee is on the property.

The security surveillance center must verify that the department leader where the vendor employee will be working has agreed to the vendor employee's presence without an escort.

It will be the sole responsibility of the leader of the restricted area to ensure the security and integrity of the area are not compromised by the vendor employee.

BADGES—TEMPORARY VISITOR BADGES

The purpose of the visitor badge is to verify and control the access of visitors to the property. Visitors' badges must be displayed at all times and are available at the security surveillance center. Security surveillance center personnel will record the following information on the visitor badge log:

Date
Visitor's name
Authorized by
Time issued
Area to visit
Security surveillance center representative signature and identification number

The badge should then be assigned a control number and issued to the visitor. Once issued, the following procedures should be followed:

- The visitor should be escorted by a department representative who is being visited.
- There should be one location for issuance and return of visitor badges.

- Visitors should be required to leave a photo ID (e.g., driver's license, employee ID, etc.) when issued a visitor badge.
- Visitor badges are considered day passes and need to be renewed on a daily basis.
- When the issued visitor badge is returned, the photo ID will be returned to the visitor.

KEY CONTROL

Key control is an important aspect and responsibility of the security surveillance center. There are many different methods and processes for the issuance, retention, and tracking of keys, badges, and other items from the security surveillance center. The following are best practices combined with guidelines and direction on one of the many ways a security surveillance center can accurately track and maintain control of these areas.

KEYS—ELECTRONIC SYSTEM

To ensure the accountability for all keys maintained and controlled by the security surveillance center, personnel will access the key box to retrieve keys using their individually assigned access code and/or access device. Authorized personnel will only be able to retrieve keys for which they have authorization. The electronic key management system records every transaction and has the ability to produce key usage logs. Continuity of the keys should be accomplished by maintaining a key control system that includes the use of an electronic key system to store keys.

KEYS—MANUAL SYSTEM

In the event that an electronic key system is unavailable, the security surveillance center personnel should use a manual key system. Security surveillance center personnel should sign keys in and out, without any exceptions. It is the responsibility of the security surveillance center personnel issuing the key to make sure that the person signing out the key writes legibly and includes his or her employee, vendor, or identification number at all times.

If the security surveillance center has an electronic key system, and it should fail to operate, a manual key log system should be maintained until the restoration of the electronic key system. The continuity of the keys should be accomplished by using a bound key control log book, which includes the following information:

- Key number
- Name, signature, and employee number of person issued key
- Date and time of the issuance of the key
- Signature and identification number of security surveillance center representative issuing key

- Date and time the key is returned to the security surveillance center key inventory
- Signature and identification number of security surveillance center representative receiving the key

KEY INVENTORY CONTROLS

A member of the security surveillance center leadership team will be responsible for the requisitioning of keys from the locksmith.

Keys received from the locksmith should be numbered and logged into inventory by a member of the security surveillance center leadership team.

NEW KEYS AND REPLACEMENT KEYS

A member of the security surveillance center leadership team will be responsible for placing any new keys into inventory and ensuring they are accounted for in the perpetual inventory.

Broken or damaged keys will be turned over to the locksmith, and replacement keys will be secured in the key box and added to the key inventory.

KEY AUDIT

A physical inventory of all security surveillance center keys will be completed periodically by a member of the security surveillance center leadership team. The perpetual inventory listed on the key log will be compared to the actual inventory of the security surveillance center keys.

If any discrepancy is found, a notation will be made in the security surveillance center key log, and a member of the security surveillance center leadership team will be notified. Every attempt will be made to determine the source of the discrepancy. If the key(s) are not located, the leader of the security surveillance center leadership team will be notified. While the location of the key is being determined, appropriate action will be taken to ensure that the respective area or lock is secured.

KEY INVENTORY

A member of the security surveillance center leadership team, at the start of each shift, will conduct an inventory of all keys.

If any discrepancy is found, a notation will be made in the log, and the leader of the security surveillance center will be notified. Every attempt will be made to determine the source of the discrepancy. While the location of the key is being determined, appropriate action will be taken to ensure that the respective area or lock is secured.

KEY DESTRUCTION

All keys that need to be replaced, due to either wear or damage, will be destroyed in the presence of a member of the security surveillance center leadership team.

RESTRICTED KEY LOG SYSTEM (MANUAL MODE)

The security surveillance center will maintain a manual key log system to be used should the electronic system fail to operate.

Continuity of the keys will be accomplished by using a bound key control log book, which includes the following information:

- Key number
- Name, signature, and employee license number of person issued key
- Date and time the key is issued
- Signature and identification number of security surveillance center representative issuing key
- Date and time the key is returned to the security surveillance center key inventory
- Signature and identification number of security surveillance center representative receiving the key

PACKAGE PASSES

When entering or exiting the property, security surveillance center personnel may examine any boxes, bags, packages, or other containers, which are under the employee's control. The contents of each container should be visually examined but not touched. The person in possession of the container may be asked to move or shift the contents to facilitate a clearer view of the interior of the container. All items departing the property that were not originally brought into the property by the individual must be accompanied by an appropriately completed package pass. All packages leaving the property should be inspected and must be accompanied by a package pass. Only the items listed on the package pass are permitted to leave the property, and the pass must be signed by the appropriate property leader.

As a rule of thumb, if a person did not bring an item onto the property, then he or she must have a package pass to leave with it.

VENDOR ROOFTOP ACCESS

Vendors are not permitted rooftop access without approval from a member of the security surveillance center leadership team. Security surveillance center personnel will verify that rooftop access has been requested and received, and persons have been properly authorized.

Authorized persons must:

- Provide personal photographic identification for verification (state, federal, or government identification).
- Provide company information and their reason for roof access.
- If the vendor is verified and identified as an authorized vendor, a 1-day temporary access badge will be issued before allowing the vendor rooftop access.
- The vendor badge must be worn the entire time the vendor is on property.

COMMUNICATION

Communicating within the security surveillance center between all personnel should be from top to bottom, bottom to top, and side to side. Communication is always important in all areas of any operation. Communication is especially important in the security surveillance center because many times, one of the first points of contact regarding life safety matters is to a member of the security surveillance center. In most instances when there is a delay in a response, it can usually be traced back to some form of communication breakdown or issue. This is a critical area because seconds could mean the difference between an excellent response to an issue or a poor resolution to an issue due to a delay in the arrival of appropriate personnel.

The following is an experience I have had in my career regarding a meeting I had prior to accepting a leadership position at a property. The senior leader of the organization advised that an area that needed to be improved upon was the communication within the department that I was going to be taking over. During my first hours in the new position, it was obvious that there was an "us" versus "them" perception between the leaders of the department and the team. Upon speaking with others, I determined that one specific area of concern was that the door leading to the leadership office was always locked and members of the team had the impression that leadership was not approachable. I addressed this with a meeting and an open discussion of areas that could be improved upon, and, of course, communication was addressed. During the meeting, to display how passionate I was about this topic, I removed the heavy metal door that led into the leadership area off of its hinges with a hammer and declared that from this moment on an open-door policy was in effect.

A very short time later, another meeting was conducted with the team. I had the department's mission statement placed on the door, and the department's open-door policy was communicated. I requested that whoever was in agreement with the mission statement and open-door policy to sign the door. Every attendee signed the door that had our mission statement boldly emblazoned on it. Of course, I was the first to sign. After the meeting, the door with the mission statement and signatures of the team was set up in the roll-call area. I attended each roll call throughout the week and explained the open-door policy to those who had not been able to attend the previous meeting. Again I requested that whoever was in agreement with the mission statement and open-door policy to sign the door. Again, every member of the team signed the door.

The door remained in the roll-call area as a visual reminder and confirmation of our department's mission statement and open-door policy. When new members joined the team, I would explain the open-door policy, the history behind the door with the mission statement and signatures, and then ask the newest addition to the team to sign the door only if the person was in agreement of the mission statement and the open-door policy. It is important that open lines of communication exist within the security surveillance center and that all members of the team value and respect the opinions, ideas, and suggestions of all, regardless of rank, title, or experience.

RADIOS

The responsibility of the issuance and operation of the radios and radio system usually is addressed by the security surveillance center. All security surveillance center personnel should be equipped with a portable radio. There are two methods that are generally utilized to distribute radios. One method is to have personnel go to a member of the security surveillance center leadership team and have a radio signed out and returned out of the radio storage/recharging area. Another method is for personnel arriving to begin their shift to retrieve the radio to be assigned to them from the person they are relieving. At the change of each shift, a member of the security surveillance center leadership team should conduct an inventory of all radios assigned to the security surveillance center. Any missing equipment should be reported immediately.

The Federal Communications Commission (FCC) sets all rules for two-way communications. All users should be familiar with the following basic rules:

- It is a violation of FCC rules to interrupt any distress or emergency message. Make sure that the line is clear before transmitting any message.
- Use of profane or obscene language is prohibited.
- It is against the law to send any false emergency message.
- All messages must be brief and limited to business needs.
- It is a violation of FCC rules to send personal messages, unless it is an emergency.
- The following phonetic alphabet should be used by the security surveillance center for all radio transmissions:

Phonetic Alphabet	
A-Alpha	N-November
B-Bravo	O-Oscar
C-Charlie	P-Papa
D-Delta	Q-Quebec
E-Echo	R-Romeo
F-Foxtrot	S-Sierra
G-Golf	T-Tango
H-Hotel	U-Uniform
I-India	V-Victor
J-Juliet	W-Whiskey
K-Kilo	X-X-Ray
L-Lima	Y-Yankee
M-Michael	Z-Zulu

ELEVATOR EMERGENCIES

In the event that there is an elevator emergency, or failure, the safety of the patrons, guests, and employees is paramount. Security surveillance center personnel should make voice contact with the occupants of the elevator via the elevator telephone system and maintain voice communication with the occupants of the elevator until they are safely released.

Security surveillance center personnel should reassure the occupants of the status of the situation, that they are safe, and that assistance is on the way. All communications should be conducted in a calm and professional manner. The security surveillance center should make the appropriate notifications and dispatch personnel to the exact location of the elevator emergency or failure.

The following processes should be completed by the appropriate department, generally the facilities or maintenance team responds to open the elevator doors. A security surveillance center representative should respond to the location and assist guests as they exit the disabled elevator.

The facilities or maintenance team should respond to the scene with an elevator emergency door key.

- If the elevator is at the proper floor level, and the doors are inoperative, a representative from the facilities or maintenance team should attempt to open the doors from the exterior of the elevator by using the elevator emergency key.
- If the elevator is between floors, and the doors are inoperative, the doors at the upper landing can be utilized for occupant removal. After the doors are opened, the doors should be wedged or blocked open to eliminate the possibility of the elevator moving. Only if it is safe to do so, a ladder can be lowered into the elevator and a representative of the facilities or maintenance team can climb into the elevator and assist the occupants up the ladder and out onto a safe area on the floor.
- In the event that the occupants of the elevator are unable to be evacuated in a reasonable amount of time, the fire department must be notified. The emergency stop button inside the elevator should be engaged whenever the emergency door key is utilized.
- The elevator company should be contacted and advised of the situation. An estimated time of arrival from the company on when a representative will be on property to make the necessary repairs should be obtained and recorded by security surveillance center personnel.

LOST AND FOUND PROCEDURES

Lost and found is a critical area at any property particularly because it addresses a level of guest service during the interaction of a property representative and the guest. It is crucial that the keepers of the lost and found area are very detail oriented and exhaust all of the established steps and methods in an attempt to reunite any lost article with the proper owner. Also, controls should be in place to ensure that the keepers of this area do not have opportunities to pilfer articles or cash in scenarios of where the person perceives a possible opportunity to steal something and get away with it. Whenever possible, you want to avoid situations where opportunity makes the thief.

All persons finding items should be directed to turn the items in to the security surveillance center, which will have the responsibility for the custody and safekeeping of the items. The security surveillance center should keep records of all articles reported to the security surveillance center as lost, found, misplaced, or missing. A member of the security surveillance center leadership team should be responsible for making sure all items have been properly secured and all reports have been completed and logged.

STORAGE AND ACCESS

Through the years, I have seen many ways that various properties stored and tracked lost and found items. Eventually, I developed the following method that worked best for me. Provided there is ample storage area, if there is not, stress the importance to executive leadership of the tracking of the lost and found items as it pertains to guest service. Once the area of storage is determined, order 31 containers that will fit in this area. The assistance of the facilities or maintenance department may be needed to build shelves, or shelves may also be ordered, on which to place the containers. The containers should be numbered 1 through 31, one storage bin for each day of the month.

On the date an item is received, it is placed into the appropriate numbered bin. For example, if an item is received on March 19, it should be placed in the bin labeled 19. When a person contacts the security surveillance center in search of an item, the date or date range the item was lost should be ascertained from the guest. The logs and appropriate bins should be inspected for the item. On the following month and date, the items should be removed from the bins and the current items for the current month and date should be placed into the appropriate bin. For example, on April 19 the items that were placed into the bin on March 19 should be removed from the bin. This is a cyclical and continuous process.

Items of high value, like cash and jewelry, should be placed in a safe.

Access to the lost and found storage room should be limited and controlled. The area should be limited to a lost and found administrator and members of the security surveillance center leadership team. If possible, a card reader should be placed on the door to track entry into the room and/or a sign-in, sign-out log should be implemented listing the name, date, time entered, and time departed. CCTV cameras should be installed in the lost and found storage area, with a camera covering the safe, another covering the exit area, and another covering the storage bins.

PROPERTY FOUND BY EMPLOYEES

Found property will be turned in to the security surveillance center. All property will be listed in the lost and found log. Garment bags, overnight bags, or suitcases should be logged, listing all of their contents. The lost and found log should contain all available information leading to the proper identification of the article or item. This information will include the following:

- Date found
- Name of the rightful owner (if known)

- Location where the item was found
- Detailed description of item

All items found on the property should be immediately turned in to the security surveillance center. Each item should be accompanied by a lost and found report. The finder of any article should immediately deliver the item to the security surveillance center where the item will be inventoried. Security surveillance center personnel should take the necessary steps to contact the rightful owner of the items found using the information available. All items of value (currency, jewelry, etc.) should be stored in a safe located in an area under the care and custody of the security surveillance center and under a CCTV surveillance camera.

When a guest claims an article at the property and the security surveillance center representative is sure of the identity, the guest will sign for the property on the lost and found report, and the following should be noted:

- Type of identification
- Identification number
- Telephone number
- Claimant's street address, city, state, and zip code

Articles will not be released without a representative of the security surveillance center leadership team being present and until the identification of the person claiming the article is confirmed and the person is verified to be the actual owner of the article.

When a lost and found article has positive identification with it, a security surveillance center representative should contact the owner of the article. This initial contact should take place over the telephone. If a telephone number cannot be obtained, the security surveillance center representative may contact the guest by mail using a form letter. When a guest wishes to claim an item, the security surveillance center representative should request an accurate description of each item from the guest.

After the articles found are clearly described, positive proof of ownership should be ascertained. The confirmed owner of the article can pick up the article or request that the article be mailed. If the guest requests that the article be mailed, the cost of postage should be paid by the guest. The article should be sent at the expense of the guest and the return portion of the receipt should be attached to the lost and found report. This information will be entered into the lost and found system, and all paperwork will be completed and filed.

When removing items from the safe, a representative of the security surveillance center leadership team will sign in the control log for the items removed. When the items are turned over to the owner of the article, the lost and found report will be signed. If the items are mailed, they will be mailed at the patron's expense and the return portion of the receipt will be attached to the lost and found report. This information will be entered into the lost and found system, and all paperwork will be completed and filed.

Telephone and mail inquiries should be handled by the security surveillance center representative in the following manner:

- An inquiry form will be completely filled out.
- The lost and found log will be checked to determine if the items were recovered.
- If the item was recovered, the guest will be informed that the article is available to be picked up or mailed at the patron's expense.
- If a guest requests to have an item of value mailed to him or her, it will be mailed with a return receipt requested.

Articles not claimed after 30 days should be given to a charitable organization. Currency should be turned over to the finance department. Employees who are finders of items should not be able to claim found items or currency. All lost and found articles not claimed, excluding cash, should be donated to a nonprofit charitable organization.

The following are general lost and found procedures, best practices, types of thefts, and tips for the prevention of losses in a lost and found environment. It is important that guests and employees perceive the facility is a place that ensures a reasonable safeguard for treatment of personal possessions.

A found item should be delivered to the lost and found area of the security surveillance center and tagged in a property bag. In situations where it is impractical for an employee to personally deliver the item, the leader of that area should be contacted to transport the item to the security surveillance center or a security surveillance center representative can be detailed to go to the location, pick up the item, and transport it back to the lost and found area of the security surveillance center.

A tracking mechanism should be utilized regarding the finding and disposition of any lost and found article. One method is to use a three-part receipt. For example, the top original sheet should be completed, and the white portion of the receipt should be retained by the security surveillance center. The middle sheet should stay with the lost and found article. The bottom sheet should be given to the person turning in the item as a receipt. Every attempt should be made to find the owner before the item is released.

The following are some areas that can be high-risk items pertaining to items and articles that are recovered, turned in to, or returned by the lost and found area of a security surveillance center.

Checkbooks

Upon receipt of a checkbook, security surveillance center personnel should ensure that all checks are in sequence, noting the starting number and ending number. If any are missing, or the checks are not in sequential order, it should be noted. When returned to the proper owner, a security surveillance center representative should review the check numbers in the checkbook with the proper owner to ensure that none of the checks have been removed.

This should be done to ensure that the guest is not a victim of a checkbook scam. How this scam works is that a check is removed from the middle or back of the checkbook by the thief. The thief writes and cashes the check stolen from the checkbook. The owner of the check usually does not discover this transaction until the withdrawal shows up on his or her bank statement. Unfortunately, many times the banks do not prosecute these types of cases due to the expenses that would be incurred, or bank insurance covers the loss.

For example, I investigated a case at a property where a hotel guest reported that she noticed a check was cashed out of sequence on her bank statement. The review of the lock interrogation report of the hotel room revealed an employee, who was recently hired, was not assigned to the room that the guest had stayed in and had entered the room a few minutes prior to the end of the shift. I obtained the job application of the employee, which was completed by the subject during the selection process, and compared the writing style and techniques to that on the check.

During the investigation, I discovered that the subject wrote the number 8 on the job application in a unique and distinctive manner. I compared this to the number 8 that appeared on the check and determined that it was identical. To make a long story short, the police were contacted, and the thief was interviewed and admitted to going into the guest room and stealing a check from the back of the guest's checkbook that was located in the guest's purse. The thief further revealed that there were others at other properties in the state who worked as a team and that they frequently stole checks from guests in this manner. The thief advised that the theft ring had stolen approximately $1 million over the course of several years and that they were rarely prosecuted when discovered.

Credit Cards

Upon receipt of a credit card, security surveillance center personnel should immediately complete the proper paperwork and secure the card. One way that a loss can occur in this area is when the credit card is received by the person in a position of trust and that person, for personal use, records the information located on the credit card prior to it being properly logged into the lost and found records. If the card is not secured properly, the credit card information has the possibility of being recorded after it has been properly logged by a rogue employee. The information gathered from the credit card can then be passed on to an accomplice who uses the card and splits the proceeds with the employee who initially obtained the information.

Other red flags in this area include the following:

- The credit card cannot be located or gets "lost" and then is rediscovered.
- The credit card is not recorded or documented as being turned in to the lost and found area.
- The credit card is not accurately recorded or documented in the destruction log.

Many times when this is discovered, the person of trust involved in this activity advises that he or she was told "that the guest was going to be stopping by to pick the card up."

A method to help to safeguard this area is to inspect the contents of trash cans in the lost and found area. For example, at a large property I worked at, I inspected the contents of the trash can used in the lost and found area and discovered pieces of completed lost and found reports that contained credit card information. After putting the pieces of the lost and found report together, it was discovered that the credit cards did not make it into the lost and found log and the person who held a position of trust admitted to taking the credit cards. The person explained that he would properly complete the paperwork but not log the credit cards into the computerized tracking system. If someone walked up and noticed the card or paperwork, the person would state that the items had to be entered. If no one noticed and the cards were not claimed by the end of the shift, the person would steal the credit cards and tear up the paperwork. This is an important area because, unfortunately, credit card fraud and expenses related to such incidents are usually passed onto the consumer in the form of increasing interest rates, service fees, and so on.

Cash

Upon receipt of cash, security surveillance center personnel should immediately complete the proper paperwork and secure the cash. One way that a loss can occur in this area is when the cash is received by the person in a position of trust and it is not recorded or logged into the lost and found records system. When this occurs, the money is usually split between the two parties involved.

Another way losses can occur in this area is when the cash is received by the person in a position of trust and it is not recorded properly or accurately. The thief records a different amount of money than what was actually turned in and steals the difference. Yet another way that money can be stolen from this area is during the reconciliation process when a person of trust lists cash as unclaimed or claimed and steals the money.

For example, I once had a leader in a position of trust take monies out of a lost and found safe and followed part of the procedure by reuniting some of the money taken from the lost and found safe to the proper owner. However, he improvised and stole other money from the safe that was not associated with the guest during the same transaction. Through an established process, procedure, checks, and balances this theft was recognized within a very short period of time and the thief was quickly dealt with.

Red Flags

- A person in a position of trust may be testing the controls and the checks and balances of the system when an item, article, or cash is received and it is not processed, recorded, or logged into the lost and found records system properly.
- If an inquiry is made pertaining to an item not processed, recorded, or logged in by the person in a position of trust, the person will commonly make claims such as the following:
  - Information was received that the guest would pick up the item, article, or cash shortly and that it was only being kept in safe keeping until the proper owner arrives.
  - The owner never showed up and the person in a position of trust "forgot" to log it into the lost and found system.
  - The person in a position of trust claims that he or she was "so busy, I forgot the item was here."

If any of the previously listed scenarios occur, the odds are that the person is testing the system and if it goes unnoticed, the item, article, or cash may be stolen the next time the opportunity presents itself.

Another technique utilized to commit theft in this area occurs when an item, article, or cash is turned into lost and found, and the person in a position of trust follows the process and procedure and properly records the item into the lost and found tracking system. The person in a position of trust in lost and found advises a conspirator of the found item, article, or cash information. The conspirator, usually on a day when the rogue employee who is in a position of trust is not working, contacts lost and found and claims the item. Frequent checks and inspections of the name, address, phone number, etc., of those claiming items will help to uncover those who claim items often. This may assist in creating a persons of interest list and can be the basis for an investigation into this area regarding specific individuals.

The following are processes that should be implemented to prevent thefts from the lost and found areas of any property:

- CCTV system cameras should be installed in the lost and found area, with a predetermined specific location for processing all paperwork and activities.
- Documentation of the entire life cycle of a lost and found item should be kept.
- Upon finding an item, article, or cash, it is to be immediately brought to the lost and found area of the security surveillance center. Personnel should immediately complete and log all paperwork and information.
- A robust, efficient, and effective property removal program should be implemented or continued.
- A stringent checks and balances program in the lost and found area should be implemented or continued.
- Reconciliation processes in the lost and found area should be implemented or continued. Any variance or discrepancy must be investigated to determine the cause.
- Separation of duties in the lost and found area must be maintained.
- In addition to regular integrity inspections, random and announced inspections should occur in the lost and found area.

It is important that security surveillance center personnel adhere to the processes in a consistent manner. Failure to do so could have catastrophic results and impact the life and safety of guests, employees, and visitors. Any time that it is observed, reported, or discovered that a member of the security surveillance center did not follow or implement a process, the situation should be addressed immediately by a member of the security surveillance center leadership team. A determination should be made on why the process was not followed and if retraining of the individual, or the entire team, should be conducted. This will help ensure the proper, effective, and efficient operation of the security surveillance center.

4 Security Surveillance Center Procedures

When developing this chapter, I was torn between providing general guidelines on security surveillance center procedures or providing in-depth, detailed procedures. As you will see, I have elected to take the detailed approach. My reasoning is that when I think back to when I first started in this field several decades ago, there were only vague, general, nonspecific, generic guidelines that I was only able to later develop into the robust procedures that you have before you today.

Strict adherence to policy and procedures is the foundation on which a successful security surveillance center relies on to be effective and efficient in any organization. The following procedures should provide a good pathway to the road for success and address many areas of those associated with the operation of security surveillance centers. Remember that procedures are living documents and should be reviewed and updated at least every 6 to 12 months. When reviewed, it is important to put in the date of revision on the procedure and to keep the old copy of procedure that was revised. This is useful for legal and performance issues to determine what procedure was in effect at the time that an incident, event, emergency, or crisis occurred.

The development of and adherence to policy and procedures are yet another method to document and exhibit professionalism, to those in the organization, and to the rest of the industry. For many reasons, it is important for all security surveillance center personnel to review and be familiar with every procedure in their area and other areas. Training and having knowledge of the other departments' standard operating procedures will aid the security surveillance center personnel to be successful. Some areas that should be focused on include the following:

- Surveillance camera techniques
- Patrols, IOUs (identify, observe, understand), and tri-shots
- Loss prevention techniques for all areas including food beverage, retail, employee areas, warehouse, and so on; audit and close watch techniques
- Standard operating procedures of all areas and departments of responsibility including security surveillance center

There is a direct correlation between the quality, thoroughness, and absorption of the standard operating procedures and how effectively and efficiently the security surveillance center will operate and respond to situations. The standard operating procedures should specify the security surveillance center's mission, objectives, and process that should be utilized to attain them. The security surveillance center's personnel need to know what is expected so that their performance can reflect meeting or exceeding the expected outcome of any incident, event, emergency, or crisis. The life, safety, and security of the organization and the internal and external guests depend on the knowledge that is exhibited by security surveillance center personnel.

The following is a format that can be used for presenting the standard operating procedures for a security surveillance center. The main thing is to ensure that the information listed below is included in the top portion or header of the document:

- Subject of standard operating procedure
- Standard operating procedure number
- Implementation date
- Revision date
- Approval—usually the leader of the security surveillance center
- Page number

The standard operating procedures should be sequentially numbered. The format should consist of an index at the beginning listing the subject and number corresponding with each standard operating procedure. Each procedure should consist of a header, which states the subject, implementation date, revision date, number, and approval. The person in charge of the security surveillance center should review every standard operating procedure and is usually the person whose name is placed in the approval section of the procedure. Although the format is important, remember the content is more critical than the format, and the absorption of the knowledge contained in standard operating procedures is key to the successful operation of any security surveillance center.

An important area of the header in the standard operating procedure is the revision date. This is very important when it comes to the operation of the team, because it indicates what policy and procedure were in place on a given date and time period. This can be critical when responding to guest complaints, performance issues, lawsuits, and the proper protection of guests, employees, and company assets.

The following are some samples of standard operating procedures that should serve as a guide to spark discussion and assist in developing property-specific departmental procedures that are standardized and assist in facilitating the professional operation of any organization.

The following are ideas and suggestions for standard operating procedures for security surveillance centers that I have found to be common denominators of any operation. These examples of standard operating procedures should provide a good backbone for your security surveillance center. Remember that standard operating procedures should keep abreast of the laws, trends, and best practices in the industry. Standard operating procedure should be crafted to meet the specific needs of your operation as issues and concerns dictate and should be reviewed by the legal branch of your organization.

STANDARD OPERATING PROCEDURE: 000
Role of Security Surveillance Center

Effective Date:
Revision Date:
Approval:

The role of the security surveillance center is to operate and maintain a closed-circuit television (CCTV) security surveillance system within the company guidelines, and it should be operated by trained personnel who conduct activities including

- Proactively protect company assets.
- Detect suspicious and criminal activity, in full cooperation with law enforcement while maintaining the integrity of the department.
- Provide protection for our internal and external guests.

The security surveillance center does not have special authority over other departments. However, the security surveillance center has an obligation to protect the company's assets by reviewing the security surveillance system for video coverage of incidents, accidents, criminal activity, policy violations, procedural violations, safety issues, and security concerns.

Security surveillance center personnel should utilize the identify, observe, and understand (IOU) method when utilizing the CCTV system. The IOU method consists of the following:

- IDENTIFY: Employees and guests in area. Identify location and assets exposed to possible loss.
- OBSERVE: Observe for signs of criminal activity and/or violation of policy/procedure.
- UNDERSTAND: Understand the observation of the activity being observed. What activities are part of the normal operation? Only when the behavior under review is normal and is not unusual or suspicious in any way should security surveillance center personnel move on to another area.
- If unusual or suspicious activity is observed, it should be monitored continuously. Monitoring should only be stopped if it is proven that the activity does not present a threat or is not a violation of the law, procedure, or policy. Once the action is determined to be a threat or a violation of the law, policy, or procedure, appropriate action should be taken.

STANDARD OPERATING PROCEDURE: 000

Equipment Usage

Effective Date:
Revision Date:
Approval:

The security surveillance center uses many tools on a daily basis to maintain the highest standards of integrity. The tools utilized include cameras, monitors, video recorders, computers, e-mail, and the communication network within the security surveillance center.

The utilization of security surveillance center equipment should be for business purposes only. At no time should equipment be utilized for personal use or in an inappropriate manner. Inappropriate uses of the security surveillance center equipment include cameras focused on the breasts, buttocks, legs, or crotch of a subject or subjects involved in private acts that do not impact the company's business or violate the law. Equipment and supplies should not be used to generate photos of celebrities, athletes, friends, associates, or family members.

The security surveillance center should emphasize the importance of proper utilization of software systems. At no time are the software systems to be used for personal use. Video recorders and printers are to be used for business purposes only. They are not to be used for personal use or to take photos of high-profile athletes, celebrities, etc.

Computer usage during working hours is for business purposes only. Communications, including e-mails, are to be professional. Any e-mail usage that may be deemed offensive (racist, sexist, vulgar, etc.) in any way is strictly prohibited and is subject to disciplinary action up to and including termination.

Items removed from the security surveillance center, including photos or videos, must have the written approval from a member of the security surveillance center leadership team.

STANDARD OPERATING PROCEDURE: 000

Access to Security Surveillance Center

Effective Date:
Revision Date:
Approval:

The security surveillance center is a secure and restricted area, and access is limited to security surveillance center personnel.

- All others must have the approval of a member of the security surveillance center leadership team.
- All visitors must sign in and sign out on the security surveillance center visitor's log. It is the responsibility of the personnel of the security surveillance center and the members of the security surveillance center leadership team who are on duty to ensure that the visitor's log is completed accurately and legibly. The log should contain the following: date, time in, time out, purpose of visit, printed name, badge number, and signature.
- Prior to any visitors entering the security surveillance center, any coverage being displayed will be turned off until the individual leaves the security surveillance center. These areas include the following: covert cameras, audits, and investigations. The purpose of this is that visitors should not have knowledge of camera coverage, locations, or any ongoing investigations.

STANDARD OPERATING PROCEDURE: 000

Chain of Command

Effective Date:
Revision Date:
Approval:

The chain of command is important to the effective operation of the security surveillance center. Any concerns, questions, complaints, requests, or issues should be directed to the immediate leader of the security surveillance center members. If the concern is not able to be resolved, the chain of command should be used, and the matter should be brought to the attention of a member of the security surveillance center leadership team.

STANDARD OPERATING PROCEDURE: 000

Code of Ethics

Effective Date:
Revision Date:
Approval:

1. Security surveillance center personnel should demonstrate a commitment to professionalism and diligence in the performance of their duties.
2. Security surveillance center personnel will not engage in any illegal or unethical conduct, or any activity that would constitute a conflict of interest.
3. Security surveillance center personnel will exhibit the highest level of integrity in the performance of all assignments.
4. Security surveillance center personnel will comply with lawful orders of the courts and will testify to matters truthfully and without bias or prejudice.
5. When reviewing coverage of an incident, investigation, and so on, security surveillance center personnel will obtain evidence or other documentation to establish the facts.
6. Security surveillance center personnel will not reveal any confidential information obtained during an assignment or investigation without the written approval of a member of the security surveillance center leadership team.
7. Security surveillance center personnel will reveal all pertinent information discovered during the course of a review or investigation.
8. Security surveillance center personnel will focus on the review, assignment, or investigation, not on the position or status of those involved.
9. Security surveillance center personnel should actively participate in the continuous learning cycle of their positions by actively seeking knowledge, participating in the training of one another, and being efficient and effective in all areas.

STANDARD OPERATING PROCEDURE: 000

Duties and Responsibilities

Effective Date:
Revision Date:
Approval:

The duties and responsibilities of security surveillance center personnel include the following:

- Ensure the relief of all personnel from the previous shift who may be on assignment. Ensure all mandatory posts are filled, previous shift personnel are relieved, and any staffing shortages are noted and recorded and a representative of the security surveillance center leadership team is notified.
- Advise all personnel whose assignments were affected by any correction, addition, or changes in posting as a result of the information supplied by a previous shift.
- Maintain a report of all pertinent activities, including responses to alarms, emergency calls, notifications, incidents, and reports involving internal or external guests.
- Custodians of keys are responsible for the control, issuing, receiving, and daily inventory of keys. These activities are to be conducted at the start and end of every shift.
- Monitor all alarm systems, respond accordingly when an alarm is received, and direct the appropriate personnel to the location of alarm activation.
- Monitor all security surveillance center equipment.
- Maintain control of all radio traffic and telephone communications that are related to the security surveillance center.
- Ensure that all paperwork is organized and completed in an accurate manner when turned over to a representative of the security surveillance center leadership team.
- The off-going security surveillance center personnel will brief the oncoming personnel regarding:
  - Operations and incidents of the last 24 hours
  - Ongoing investigations, incidents, and assignments
  - Information concerning internal and external guests, investigations, and any suspicious or criminal activity
  - All other pertinent information
- Security surveillance center personnel must familiarize themselves with the operations, information, and incidents that occurred during their days off.

- Cameras and equipment will be checked for proper placement and function on a daily basis.
- Playbacks and time/date checks will be performed on a daily basis.
- Any discrepancies will be communicated to a representative of the security surveillance center leadership team as soon as possible.
- When observing unusual, suspicious, or criminal activity, a triangulated camera setup (tri-shot) is required to observe and document the activity. Additional coverage and cameras may be used, but a tri-shot is the minimum coverage that must be maintained. The tri-shot camera setup will be maintained until the activity is resolved.
- Falsification, alteration, deletion, or omission of any information with intent to falsify the reporting of an incident, event, etc., is considered to be an act of gross misconduct and is subject to disciplinary action, up to and including termination.
- Removal of any items from the security surveillance center is permitted with written approval from a member of the security surveillance center leadership team.
- Security surveillance center personnel will treat all information confidentially and will maintain a high level of integrity.
- Security surveillance center personnel may not release any information regarding any surveillance activity, equipment, or extent of camera coverage without written permission from a member of the security surveillance center leadership team.
- The highest-ranking representative of the security surveillance center leadership team must be kept informed of the actions and communications security surveillance center personnel have with other departments.
- Security surveillance center personnel must log all pertinent and required information in a complete, accurate, and timely manner.

STANDARD OPERATING PROCEDURE: 000

Key Control

Effective Date:

Revision Date:

Approval:

The purpose of the key control system is to ensure adequate accountability for all keys maintained and controlled by the security surveillance center.

- All keys maintained and controlled by the security surveillance center for issuance will be secured in a lockable container within the security surveillance center. Access to the lockable storage container will only be accessible by the designated members of the security surveillance center leadership team.

- The maintenance of the keys will be kept by using a bound ledger book to ensure the continuity of the keys. Information recorded in the key control log should consist of the following:
  - Date and time key is signed out
  - Signature and employee number of the receiving employee
  - Name and employee number of the issuing security surveillance center representative
  - Signature and employee number of employee returning key
  - Signature and employee number of security surveillance center representative receiving key
  - Date and time key returned

Daily Inventory of Keys

- A member of the security surveillance center leadership team will, at the start of each shift, take an inventory of all keys.
- If any discrepancy is found, a notation will be made in the log, and the leader of the security surveillance center will be notified. Every attempt will be made to determine the source of the discrepancy.
- If the key cannot be located, the leader of the security surveillance center will notify executive leadership. While the location of the key is being determined, appropriate action will be taken to ensure that the respective area or lock is secured.

Physical Key Audits

- A physical inventory of all keys will be completed periodically at the direction of the leader of the security surveillance center by a member of the security surveillance center leadership team. The perpetual inventory listed on the security surveillance center key log will be compared to the actual inventory of the keys maintained by the security surveillance center.
- If any discrepancy is found, a notation will be made on the key log and a member of the security surveillance center will be immediately notified. Every attempt will be made to determine the source of the discrepancy. If the key is unable to be located, the leader of the security surveillance center will notify executive leadership. While the location of the key is being determined, appropriate action will be taken to ensure that the respective area or lock is secured.

New Keys and Replacement Keys

- A member of the security surveillance center leadership team will be responsible for placing any new keys into the inventory and ensuring that they are accounted for in the perpetual inventory.

- A member of the security surveillance center leadership team will be responsible for obtaining keys from the locksmith.
- All new keys and replacement keys will be numbered and logged into inventory by a member of the security surveillance center leadership team.
- A key request form will be completed and turned over to a member of the security surveillance center leadership team.

Key Destruction

- All keys that need to be replaced due to wear or damage will be reported to a member of the security surveillance center leadership team.
- The key will be destroyed in the presence of a member of the security surveillance center leadership team, and the information will be recorded in the daily activity log.
- Broken or damaged keys will be turned over to a member of the security surveillance center leadership team.
  - All pieces of the broken key are to be turned over to a member of the security surveillance center leadership team.
  - If all the pieces of the key are returned, a replacement key can be requested.
  - If all the pieces of the key are not returned, the leader of the security surveillance center will be notified and a determination will be made regarding if the respective area or lock needs to be secured and/or replaced.

Lost Keys

- Lost keys will be immediately reported to a member of the security surveillance center leadership team.
- The leader of the security surveillance center will be immediately notified and will determine if the lock associated with the lost key needs to be replaced.

STANDARD OPERATING PROCEDURE: 000
Issuing of Temporary Badges

Effective Date:
Revision Date:
Approval:

Security surveillance center personnel is to verify and control access to the facility by the issuance, tracking, and collection of access badges into controlled areas of the property. The following are the types of badges that the security surveillance center is responsible for maintaining, tracking, and destroying.

- Employee temporary access badge
- Nonemployee temporary access badge
- Vendor temporary access badge
- Contractor temporary access badge

Requestors of temporary badges will report to the security surveillance center badging booth area and request a temporary badge. A member of the security surveillance center team will:

- Contact the immediate supervisor of the employee requesting the badge and verify employment.
- If unable to confirm with requestor's immediate supervisor, a member of the security surveillance center leadership team will be contacted to verify employment.
- If requestor is not actively employed, will not be issued.
- Inform the requestor to call the supervisor or department that he or she wishes to access and schedule an appointment.
- If the requestor is actively employed, confirm identification, request to see picture ID from requestor.
- If identification is confirmed, a temporary access badge should be issued to the area(s) the requestor is authorized to have access to.
- Advise the requestor that the access badge must be displayed at all times and that the badge must be returned to the security surveillance center upon exiting the property.
- The following information will be documented into the access badge log:
  - Date issued
  - Time issued
  - Requestor's first name, last name, and employee number
  - Authorized by (first and last names)
  - Location to be accessed
  - Positon
  - Issuing security surveillance center personnel first name, last name, and employee number

---

STANDARD OPERATING PROCEDURE: 000

Service Expectations

Effective Date:
Revision Date:
Approval:

The security surveillance center will consistently and efficiently provide exceptional service. The security surveillance center will continually strive to develop and nurture relationships with the emergency response agencies, law enforcement, and internal and external guests without compromising the integrity of the security surveillance center operation. This will be accomplished by establishing and providing the following as the minimum service that will be provided.

- During the interaction with others on the phone, radio, or in person, security surveillance center personnel will be polite, courteous, and professional at all times.
- When a request for assistance is received, security surveillance center personnel will do the following:
  - Provide assistance in a timely and efficient manner.
  - Provide an update to the requestor as quickly and accurately as possible regarding whether the security surveillance center will be handling the request, who will be the security surveillance center point of contact during the course of the investigation or response, and the time frame of when the request will be completed.
  - The release of confidential or sensitive information will only be disseminated to authorized individuals, with the approval of a member of the security surveillance center leadership team and only on a need-to-know basis.
  - Follow up with the requestor of information to ensure that assistance was received and concerns were addressed.
  - Any requests that are unable to be completed must be communicated to the next shift and leadership of the security surveillance center.
  - CCTV reviews will be thorough, accurate, and complete. Security surveillance center personnel will exhaust all leads prior to terminating any review or investigation.
  - Incident reports should be completed prior to the end of the shift. Reports will immediately be placed on the report log and an incident report number will be assigned. In the event that an incident is continued into the next shift, the report will be updated with the known information. This will continue until the report is up-to-date and the investigation is completed.
  - At shift change, the leadership of the outgoing shift of the security surveillance center will brief the oncoming shift thoroughly. All pertinent information will be passed on to the oncoming shift, including entries, reports, and incidents.
  - Security surveillance center personnel will ensure that they are thoroughly familiar with all information developed, obtained or incidents that have occurred since the last time they worked in the security surveillance center.

STANDARD OPERATING PROCEDURE: 000

Employee Hotline

Effective Date:
Revision Date:
Approval:

The implementation of employee hotline aids in the reporting and identification of those who may be verifying company policy. Procedures of the law when a report of information is received on the employee hotline, the security surveillance center response should include the following:

- Hotline calls are documented and a report is generated and sent to members of the security surveillance center leadership team.
- The security surveillance center will investigate hotline calls that are related to the security surveillance center areas of responsibility.
- The leadership in the security surveillance center will
  - Ensure that a review of coverage of the area of an alleged incident occurs in a timely manner.
  - Assign investigations and reviews to a specific member of the security surveillance center.
  - Immediately save all CCTV coverage for review.
  - When needed, generate a case file and incident report.
  - Any issues or concerns that may arise during an investigation are to be brought to the attention of a member of the security surveillance leadership team.
  - Ensure that the outcomes of the findings of a review/investigation are completed, and appropriate actions and notifications are made accordingly.

STANDARD OPERATING PROCEDURE: 000

Relief and Shift Change

Effective Date:
Revision Date:
Approval:

Security surveillance center personnel will include the following during relief of assignment, post, and shift changes:

- At the beginning of each shift, the oncoming security surveillance center member(s) will be briefed by the previous shift of any incidents, investigations, or activities.

- Prior to the end of the shift, the security surveillance center personnel to be relieved are to ensure that the security surveillance center is left clean and clear of paperwork, trash, and personal items.
- Security surveillance center personnel will prepare the reports, conduct a camera inspection, and document the inspection and any discrepancies found.
- Security surveillance center personnel will inspect the life safety and access control systems to ensure all are working properly.
- Security surveillance center personnel will monitor the CCTV system to ensure the safety, security, and protection of the company's assets.
- Any, discrepancies, or equipment failures are to be reported to a member of the security surveillance center immediately.

STANDARD OPERATING PROCEDURE: 000

Daily Activity Report

Effective Date:
Revision Date:
Approval:

The daily activity report is utilized to maintain, store, track, and search the daily activities of the security surveillance center. The daily activity report entries should include the following:

- Requests, reports, observations, or notifications that may require a response from the security surveillance center (when in doubt, make an entry)
- Any pertinent information received
- Any unusual or suspicious activity reported or observed
- Any reviews or investigations
- When the security surveillance center system malfunctions or is repaired
- When state, local, or federal authorities are contacted, arrive on property, or have communications with the security surveillance center
- When the security surveillance center is entered by any outside agency or person (a detailed explanation must be entered)

Log entries should contain all pertinent information, including date, time, location, details, personnel involved, and departments involved. When possible, the following information pertaining to an event will be entered and these will be answered: who, what, when, where, why, and how.

STANDARD OPERATING PROCEDURE: 000

Logs and Documentation

Effective Date:
Revision Date:
Approval:

The following process should be followed when maintaining an accurate log to create effective and appropriate documentation of an action, incident, or report.

Logs and documentation are designed to maintain an accurate record of actions, incidents, and reports. They must be maintained in a thorough, professional, and accurate manner. The security surveillance center uses and maintains numerous types of logs, including

- Shift logs
- Lost and found logs
- Key control logs
- Visitor logs
- Vehicle logs
- Incident report logs

These logs should always be accurate and up-to-date. It is essential that the recording of all events occurs immediately and is referenced in the appropriate log.

- All logs are to be maintained on a continuous basis.
- Each security surveillance center member is responsible for the area and logs that are assigned to the area.
- Log entries must be accurate, concise, and thorough.
- The security surveillance center member making a log entry must complete that entry, to the best of his or her ability, and sign off on the entry.

STANDARD OPERATING PROCEDURE: 000

Incident Reports

Effective Date:
Revision Date:
Approval:

A report narrative is the essence of an incident report. It provides the reader with the details of an incident. Generally, a report narrative should contain an introductory paragraph, an investigative paragraph, an action paragraph, an optional notifications paragraph, and a disposition paragraph.

- The introductory section serves as the introduction to a report narrative. It should briefly state when and where an incident was observed or first reported and briefly give an overview of the incident.
- If the report is a request, list the name and title of the person making the request and the nature of the request (i.e., video review, request for coverage, etc.).
- The investigative section states the details of the incident and what the report writer observed during the course of the incident. The information should be provided in an accurate and chronological manner of what occurred. This section should be very detailed and answer the questions who, what, when, where, why, and how.
- The action section states what actions were taken immediately following the investigation or observation. It is a follow-up to the investigative section.
- The notifications section lists who was contacted regarding the incident. This would include persons who must be contacted per policy (i.e., security surveillance center leader, etc.).
- The disposition section closes the report. It should include disposition of the incident video and items attached with the report (i.e., witness statements, etc.), or if the case is to be forwarded to another department or agency for further investigation.

The following are guidelines for writing a good report narrative:

- Report only the facts.
- Never speculate, give opinion, or report hearsay.
- The report must be factual and unbiased. Security surveillance center personnel should be mindful that the reader did not witness the incident and is relying on the investigator to paint a factual, concise, complete, and accurate picture of the incident. As the fictional character, Detective Sergeant Joe Friday from the program *Dragnet* is credited with saying, "just the facts" are all that is reported.
- Information gathering is a key element in the writing of any good report. Gather as much information as possible about the incident from any witness or people involved. Information not needed can always be omitted, but you may never get a second chance to go back and get information from a witness or people involved in the incident that is needed for your report. Remember to answer who, what, when, where, why, and how.
- Subjects listed in the report should always be listed with their title, first name, and last name, the first time they appear in the report. Any additional times the person appears in the report, only his or her last name should be used, and it should be capitalized. In the event that two or more people in the report have the same last name, refer to them by first initial and last name after they are initially introduced with their full name and title.

- Unknown or unidentified persons should be listed with a description of the subject by race, gender, approximate age, clothing description, any other notable characteristics, and should be referred to as unidentified or unknown subject 1, unidentified or unknown subject 2, and so on.
- Security surveillance center personnel should write the report in third person. This makes it easier for the reader to understand, especially when the report is being read by outside agencies, lawyers, judges, etc.
- Who, what, when, where, why, and how should be answered in a report.
- Organize the report by using paragraphs with proper punctuation and capitalization.
- Abbreviations that first appear in a report must be fully spelled out followed by the abbreviation in parentheses.
- Every report must be proofread by the writer, and the spell-checked program must be utilized and corrections, if needed, made.
- Reports will be given to a member of the security surveillance center leadership team. The leader will proofread the report, direct any changes as needed, and initial or print name in the lower right-hand corner of the final report. Once the review is completed, the report can be distributed—with proper authorization.
- Remember incident reports are official documents that are often viewed by many different people and agencies, including outside departments, top leadership in an organization, and law enforcement agencies. In some cases, incident reports may be subpoenaed for criminal or civil litigation.

STANDARD OPERATING PROCEDURE: 000

Hold-up Alarm

Effective Date:

Revision Date:

Approval:

When an alarm is received, the security surveillance center personnel will view the alarm location area on the CCTV display. The security surveillance center personnel will, if known, announce the nature of the alarm: actual, malfunction, or requires an investigation.

Security surveillance center personnel handling this assignment will observe entrance/exit locations for likely suspects, determine if the area is safe to approach, and report observations to representatives of the security surveillance center leadership team.

Security surveillance center personnel will use appropriate cameras and monitors to locate and identify suspects and/or reason for alarm.

ACTUAL EVENT

- Advise a member of the security surveillance center leadership team.
- Monitor suspects and situation until situation is resolved and a representative of the security surveillance center leadership team advises that coverage of the event has been terminated.
- Maintain radio contact with responding security personnel with all pertinent information and immediately report if area is, or has become, unsafe to approach.
- The security surveillance center will immediately contact law enforcement and provide pertinent information; advise if subjects are on or off property; if weapons are involved, number of suspects, description, direction of travel, vehicle description, and so on.
- Retain pertinent video coverage as evidence. Complete a log entry and an incident report.

ACCIDENTAL ALARM OR ALARM MALFUNCTION

- Advise a member of the security surveillance center leadership team.
- Monitor alarm location and situation until situation is resolved and a representative of the security surveillance center leadership team advises that coverage of the event has been terminated.
- Maintain radio contact with responding security surveillance center personnel with all pertinent information.
- Ensure alarm is reset.

Every alarm activation should be treated as an actual event. For the safety of responding personnel, a complete review of the alarm location and surrounding areas should be conducted prior to sending anyone to the scene. If weapons are observed, law enforcement must be contacted immediately. When serious events occur, timely and accurate information is to be provided to law enforcement.

STANDARD OPERATING PROCEDURE: 000

Criminal Activity

Effective Date:
Revision Date:
Approval:

When criminal activity is detected or reported, the highest-ranking representative of the security surveillance center leadership team should be contacted immediately, and the steps taken should include the following:

- Tri-shot coverage of the activity should occur.
- A determination of the event must be made as to whether it is an actual crime in progress. Ascertain if the perpetrator(s) is still on property.
- If unable to verify that a crime has occurred or that reasonable cause has not been established that a crime has been committed, then the investigation must continue until it can be proven. Only after there is undisputed video evidence that a crime has been committed and the perpetrator(s) can be clearly identified by video evidence should subjects be detained.
- If the suspect(s) departs the property, gather all video evidence of the incident and prepare a package for law enforcement. Information gathered for law enforcement should include the following:
  - CCTV coverage
  - Photos of suspects
  - Vehicle description
  - License number
  - Any other pertinent information
- Notify the appropriate law enforcement agency of the incident.
- Prepare necessary statements and incident reports.

STANDARD OPERATING PROCEDURE: 000

Evidence

Effective Date:
Revision Date:
Approval:

The steps taken regarding evidence should include the following:

- CCTV recordings generated in the course of an investigation should be saved as evidence.
- The occasions when video evidence should be retained include criminal activity, suspected criminal activity, suspensions, suspension pending investigation, termination, violation of policy, violation of procedure, suspicious activity, and when additional investigation and/or review will be performed.
- When an incident report is issued, its associated CCTV recordings should be listed as evidence within the report.
- CCTV video recordings should be made of all significant incidents and should include coverage of 10 minutes prior to the incident and 10 minutes after the incident.
- The label on a CCTV recordings should include the incident report number, date of incident, time of incident, short description of the incident, name of suspect, and incident report number.
- The labeled CCTV recording should be stored in the designated evidence storage location, and the item should be entered into the evidence log.
- A representative of the security surveillance center leadership team should assigned the evidence custodian.

STANDARD OPERATING PROCEDURE: 000

Technicians

Effective Date:
Revision Date:
Approval:

The maintenance and repair of the security surveillance center system is paramount for the effective and efficient operation of the security surveillance center. Technicians should be assigned on a regular and consistent basis for the routine repair and maintenance of the security surveillance center's CCTV equipment. These duties include the following:

- Repair/replacement of the security surveillance center equipment, system, and components.
- Routine cleaning and maintenance of the security surveillance center equipment, system, and components.
- Adherence to a developed maintenance program of all of the security surveillance center equipment, system, and components.
- Synchronization of security surveillance center equipment, system, and components with time and date generators. Verify that the synchronization of these systems matches other key areas where times and dates are used by employees (i.e., time clocks, telephones, cash registers, etc.).
- Review special projects and installations with members of the leadership team of the security surveillance center to ensure that they are communicated clearly, planned, budgeted, scheduled, approved, and authorized.
- All equipment and parts needed for repairs, maintenance, or special projects will be reviewed with a member of the leadership team of the security surveillance center. Only after approval has been granted will a purchase order be generated and submitted.
- It will be the responsibility of the security surveillance center technicians to ensure that all equipment and parts ordered are received as scheduled.
- Any items not received as scheduled will immediately be brought to the attention of a member of the leadership team of the security surveillance center.
- All items, equipment, systems, and components will be audited on a periodic basis. Any discrepancies will immediately be reported to a member of the leadership team of the security surveillance center.

STANDARD OPERATING PROCEDURE: 000

CCTV Response to Malfunctions

Effective Date:
Revision Date:
Approval:

The following procedures are to be implemented in the event that the security surveillance center should experience malfunctions or a failure of the system.

For the purpose of this procedure, a security surveillance center malfunction and failure are defined as follows:

- *Malfunction*: When the CCTV cameras or CCTV system are not operating at their peak capacity but are still operational and able to provide coverage as needed.

- *Failure*: When the CCTV cameras or CCTV system becomes completely disabled.
- When either event occurs, a member of the security surveillance center leadership must be notified immediately.
- When either event occurs, repairs must begin immediately. If it is determined that outside resources are needed, the technician will explain the situation and what is needed to a member of the security surveillance center leadership team. Once approved by leadership, vendors will be contacted and any other sources needed to expedite the repairs will be contacted.
- All vendors, contractors, and outside sources will follow the proper visitor procedures and will be escorted to all restricted areas. A member of the security surveillance center will remain in physical proximity with the visitor while on property and until the visitor's departure.
- If the malfunction or failure impacts the operation of dedicated cameras in cash handling areas or high-risk areas such as cash control, the repairs must begin immediately and additional security measures should be taken.
- If repairs are unable to be made and additional security measures cannot be implemented, the affected area may have to be shut down until repairs are completed or additional security measures are instituted.
- Security surveillance center personnel must report malfunctions or failures to a member of the security surveillance center leadership team. The security surveillance center leader will notify executive leadership.
- Security surveillance center personnel will document all camera or system malfunctions or failures.
- General and routine repair and maintenance will be performed on a consistent basis. Repair logs and other pertinent reports that pertain to the effectiveness of the CCTV system will be reviewed daily. Any areas or items identified as not working properly will be repaired as quickly as possible.
- Requests for necessary repair parts or replacement equipment must be submitted to the leader of the security surveillance center immediately. This will ensure the prompt repair or replacement of any security surveillance center CCTV equipment.

STANDARD OPERATING PROCEDURE: 000

Employee Incidents

Effective Date:
Revision Date:
Approval:

When observations occur of incidences when something "just doesn't look right," determinations of exactly what is being observed and the processes that should be implemented include the following:

- A representative of the security surveillance center leadership team should be contacted immediately. A determination should be made if the violation involves criminal activity, or is a violation of policy or procedure.
- If it is determined the criminal activity, or a violation of policy or procedure occurred then appropriate action should be taken.
- At the time of the violation, ascertain the location of the employee's supervisor.
- Report the violation to the appropriate department head.
- If necessary, review the video recording with the department head.
- Enter the incident into the daily log and complete an incident report.

STANDARD OPERATING PROCEDURE: 000

Inspection of Items

Effective Date:

Revision Date:

Approval:

This policy is intended for those security surveillance centers that are located at the main entrance of a property or areas where employees are required to enter and exit. This program can be implemented when persons are entering or exiting the property with any type of container or bag. A designated window should be designated for the bag checks with a specific camera assigned to this location. Check with company policy and keep abreast of the law regarding the inspection of containers and bags as it relates to the Fourth Amendment. The basic rule of thumb is that once inspections are started, they should continue until there is a break of no more people in line. Another method used is to pick a random number, say three, and check the bags of every third person who enters the location at the security surveillance center. Once again, only stop the inspections after there are no more people in line.

- For the purposes of this policy, containers and bags include the following items: purses, backpacks, bags, duffels, boxes, or any other form of container.
- For employees, check and make sure that words to the effect are written in the company handbook—all employees are required to allow a representative of the security surveillance center to examine any boxes, bags, packages, or other containers that are under their control when entering or exiting the property. For nonemployees, check and make sure that there is a sign displayed and clearly posted outside of the security surveillance center that specifies that all containers are subject to inspection upon arrival or departure from the property.

When conducting an inspection, security surveillance center personnel should visually examine the contents of each container. At no time is an item in the container to be touched or moved by any member of the security surveillance center. If the security surveillance center personnel would like an item being inspected to be moved, the person in possession of the container can be asked to move or shift the contents in order to allow for a clearer view of the interior of the container. All items departing the property that were not originally brought into the property by an individual must be accompanied by a properly completed package pass.

- If an employee refuses to have his or her items searched, a member of the security surveillance center leadership team should speak with the person and remind him or her that the employee handbook specifies that participation of container inspections is required. If the employee refuses to participate in the inspection, the employee is to be advised that a report will be written and a copy will be given to their department leader and to the department of human resources.
- If a nonemployee refuses to participate in the inspection, a member of the security surveillance center leadership team is to review the sign displayed and clearly posted outside of the security surveillance center that specifies that all containers are subject to inspection upon arriving or departing from the property. If the person continues to refuse to participate, a member of the security surveillance center leadership team will advise the person that a trespass notice will be issued and the person will not be permitted onto the property until further notice.
- Any item belonging to the property discovered during the inspection of items that is not accompanied by a property package pass is to be thoroughly investigated. A rule of thumb is that a property pass is needed for the removal of anything leaving the property that was not brought to property by the remover.
- In any case where a subject refuses to participate in the inspection of items, or items are discovered that belong to the property and are unaccompanied by a package pass, the following are to be completed:
  - CCTV coverage will be obtained, saved, and stored.
  - Statements will be obtained from witnesses and those security surveillance center members involved in the inspection of items.
  - A member of the security surveillance center leadership team will complete a written report.
  - The information pertaining to the incident will be forwarded to the appropriate areas.

In all cases where an incident report must be written. The CCTV video recordings of the area where the request for inspection occurred, for the time period inclusive of this incident, will be secured in a timely manner.

STANDARD OPERATING PROCEDURE: 000

Dissemination of Information

Effective Date:
Revision Date:
Approval:

- When the security surveillance center receives information from law enforcement, informants, and other sources, it needs to be disseminated in a timely manner.
- A representative of the security surveillance center leadership team will make the determination as to who should receive the information and when the information will be distributed.
- When information is disseminated, clearly establish that it is alleged/reported information. Only when the event and the information have been verified, and it is proven that the event/incident has actually occurred, can it be disseminated as fact.

STANDARD OPERATING PROCEDURE: 000

Photos

Effective Date:
Revision Date:
Approval:

The steps that security surveillance center personnel are to follow when releasing authorized photos include the following:

- Only photos needed for company business will be taken.
- When a photo is released, an entry is required in the log.
- A member of the security surveillance center leadership team must approve the release of any photos.
- When a photo is released, outside the department, a copy of that photo should be retained and filed in the security surveillance center.
- A security surveillance center photograph release form must be completed.

STANDARD OPERATING PROCEDURE: 000

Performance Expectations

Effective Date:
Revision Date:
Approval:

The following are the performance expectations of all security surveillance center personnel:

- Be calm, polite, courteous, and professional at all times.
- Check equipment at the start of every shift to ensure all is functioning properly.
- Provide assistance in a thorough, accurate, complete, efficient, and timely manner.
- When cameras are not in use, they must be placed in their designated programmed positions.
- Monitor for suspicious activities, including loitering. Loiterers may be lookouts, scoping the area for a future crime or waiting to commit crimes of opportunity.
- Properly receive and record all alarms and take appropriate action.
- Check all access control systems, fire command center equipment/life safety equipment, and CCTV equipment. Make sure all are in proper working order. Any malfunctions or anomalies must immediately be reported to a member of the security surveillance center leadership team and noted in the daily log.
- The CCTV system will be monitored to ensure the safety of the property, company assets, and the safety and security of the internal and external guests.
- The setup and display of the CCTV system should be dictated by property needs, past experiences, types of incidents, and event types.
- For the protection of the internal and external customer, coverage should be established at the entrances, exits, back of house, and high-volume, high-traffic, and event areas.
- All violations of policy and procedure should be investigated to determine if they were done in error or with malicious intent. Violations can be indicators of theft or other criminal behavior.
- Beverages are not permitted on the console.
- If beverages are permitted in the security surveillance center, they are to have covers on the containers.
- Personal phone calls are not permitted from the security surveillance center.
- The security surveillance center is to be cleaned before the end of every shift.

- All paperwork will be reviewed for accuracy and thoroughness prior to the completion of the shift.
- Briefing and information are to be exchanged between security surveillance center personnel at the start of the shift and when relieved.
- When transmitting information via the radio, security surveillance center personnel will remain polite, calm, and professional at all times.
- Incident reports must be completed prior to the end of the shift. In the event that an incident is continued to the next shift, an incident report will be opened and the known information listed within the report. If necessary, the next shift will complete the report or bring it up-to-date until the investigation is completed.
- Security surveillance center personnel will thoroughly brief the oncoming shift on all pertinent information including entries, reports, and incidents.
- All security surveillance center personnel will thoroughly familiarize themselves with all information developed or obtained from the previous 24 hours or since they last worked.

STANDARD OPERATING PROCEDURE: 000

Telephone Communications

Effective Date:
Revision Date:
Approval:

A best practice is to have regular telephone numbers and an emergency telephone number in the security surveillance center. The following are the telephone communication procedures to be adhered to by all security surveillance center personnel.

All nonemergency telephone calls will be answered within three rings, with the following salutation:

"Good (Morning/Afternoon/Evening). Security surveillance center, (name) speaking. How may I assist you?"

No jargon/slang is to be used. If the telephone has the capability of displaying caller information, observe the telephone number, name, or room for easy reference and aid in calling back. If information does not appear, request this information from the caller.

If the guest has the wrong number, assist by doing one of two things:

- Assist and transfer the call personally step by step.
- Call the proper department for the guest and relay the message.

When transferring a call, inform the recipient of the caller's request before the transfer is complete.

Always thank the person for calling.

When taking messages, always write the following legibly:

- Caller's last name, first name
- Caller's phone number
- Day and time of the call
- Person requested
- Message
- Your initials

Prior to ending the call, repeat all information back to the caller to confirm that it is accurate. When placing a caller on hold, always ask, "May I place you on a brief hold?" Callers should be given the opportunity to respond before they are placed on hold.

Personal calls are not permitted, with the exception of emergency calls.

When calls are received on the emergency line, the call will be answered immediately, with the following message:

"Emergency Line—What is your emergency?"

Any caller who does not have an actual emergency should be advised that the line they have called is only for emergency calls. The nonemergency extension number should be provided, and the caller should be directed to hang up and call that extension.

- Phone etiquette—Answer the telephone within three rings in the following manner:
    - Between 2400 and 1200 hours—"Good morning, this is [YOUR NAME] of the security surveillance center. How may I assist you?"
    - Between 1200 and 1700 hours—"Good afternoon, this is [YOUR NAME] of the security surveillance center. How may I assist you?"
    - Between 1700 and 2400 hours—"Good evening, this is [YOUR NAME] of the security surveillance center. How may I assist you?"

Closing of Any Telephone Call

- Ask if there is anything else that you can help the caller with. If the person does not need any further assistance, end the call with "Thank you, it has been my pleasure speaking with you."

STANDARD OPERATING PROCEDURE: 000

Property Removal

Effective Date:
Revision Date:
Approval:

Employees are not authorized to remove company property from the facility without written approval from an authorized member of the leadership team.

- When an employee has a cause to remove property from the facility, the employee must receive written authorization (in the form of a property clearance form) from an authorized member of the leadership team.
- This property clearance form is to be filled out by an authorized member of the leadership team, indicating the materials/articles to be removed. This form will also contain the authorized member of the leadership team's signature and title.
- Prior to the employee departing the property with an item, the employee must first stop at the security surveillance center public window and present the item and property clearance form.
- The property clearance form, along with the item, will be inspected, and the signature on the property clearance form will be compared to the authorized leadership team master clearance signature list. If the item is listed and the signature is cleared, then the security surveillance center personnel who inspected the package pass and item will sign the form, and retain. The form will be turned over to a member of the security surveillance center leadership team and then filed.

Upon exiting or entering the property, the company reserves the right to inspect all items, including packages, parcels, and bags. Security surveillance center personnel will not place hands inside of any container. In the circumstance where there is an obstruction, the security surveillance center representative will ask the person to move the item. Package checks should always be in view of the CCTV camera system. Employees and vendors are to always use authorized entrances and exits. If an employee or vendor is observed exiting the facility from an unauthorized exit, the employee or vendor is to be stopped and items are to be inspected in view of the CCTV camera system.

PACKAGE PASS INSPECTION GUIDELINES

- All items removed from the facility must adhere to strict guidelines and have approval from an authorized member of the leadership team.
- A rule of thumb is that if you did not bring it in, you must have a package pass to leave with it.

- Upon leaving the building, all employees will make all items (personal bags, boxes, briefcases, etc.) available for inspection by the security surveillance center. Package inspections are to be done on everyone in a polite and courteous manner.
- Items purchased from the facility stores do not need a package pass as long as a receipt for all items being removed from the property accompanies items. (Remember when checking the receipt to verify the items, quantity, date, and time.)
- A package pass will be required for all items that are leaving the facility. All items must be listed and accompanied by a package pass, which must be approved by an authorized member of the leadership team listed on the package pass authorized signature list.

STANDARD OPERATING PROCEDURE: 000

Active Shooter

Effective Date:
Revision Date:
Approval:

Having been involved in a shooting where I was shot six times in one incident in 1989 as a New Jersey State Trooper. I have passed on my personal experience regarding being involved in a shooting incident to various law enforcement agencies across the country and have presented on the topic to a variety of audiences.

I thought carefully before placing this procedure in the book. One of the main reasons is that I did not want to place material in the book that was not part of the day-to-day operations of a security surveillance center. However, in light of recent events, random shootings at businesses of all kinds, the increase of terrorist activity throughout the world and on our homeland, I feel obligated to provide a procedure to you in the event that a situation of this magnitude should arise.

The purpose of the active shooter procedure is to identify the role of the security surveillance center if such an event should occur. The following guidelines cannot cover every possible situation that might occur, but they serve as an awareness and tool with the goal to reduce the number of injuries or deaths if such a situation should develop. Active shooter events cannot be predicted to follow any pattern; therefore, the following protocol should act as a possible sequencing guideline for this type of situation:

- When the security surveillance center receives information that shots have been fired, 911 will be contacted immediately. Be prepared for the emergency phone system to be overwhelmed when this type of event occurs.
- Security surveillance center personnel should remain calm and speak in a clear manner.

- When a call is received and/or information of the call is communicated, the location of the event will immediately be brought up on CCTV system, and all areas will be scanned in an effort to answer who, what, when, where, why, and how. Some of the information that should be gathered includes:
  - What is happening
  - Where the caller is located, including building name and room numbers
  - Description and number of people at the caller's specific location
  - Types of weapons
  - Any injuries—how many people are injured and types of injuries
  - Caller's name and callback phone number
- Appropriate notifications will be made.
- All security surveillance center personnel should continue to perform their duties during this type of event as long as it is safe to do so. The security surveillance center is a key component in providing critical information to responding law enforcement and emergency response agencies.
- Only if it is safe to do so, the appropriate personnel will be dispatched to evacuate guests and employees to a safe area and await the arrival of law enforcement.
- For those in areas that are unsafe to evacuate, steps should be taken for proactive cover.
- Communication between the security surveillance center, responding personnel, law enforcement, and emergency response agencies is critical during and after this type of event.
- Up-to-date information regarding the event is critical to those responding and must be communicated accurately. This information includes the identification, location, and actions of the perpetrator(s).
- CCTV coverage of the incident is critical. The shooter may flee when law enforcement arrives or might shoot at responding law enforcement agencies.
- Remember active shooter situations demand an immediate response to the situation by law enforcement to stop the shooting and prevent further harm. The goal is for the security surveillance center to assist law enforcement to locate, contain, and stop the shooter(s).
- Remember that injured persons will not be treated until the shooter is neutralized and the area is secure.
- Once the threat is neutralized, law enforcement will begin evacuations and emergency responders will begin the treatment of the injured.
- For situations such as this, and other types of emergency situations, it is a good idea for all employees to program the property security surveillance center emergency phone number into their cell phones.

STANDARD OPERATING PROCEDURE: 000
Heightened Security Surveillance Center Alert

Effective Date:
Revision Date:
Approval:

HEIGHTENED SECURITY SURVEILLANCE CENTER ALERT PROCEDURES

The purpose of this heightened security procedure is to increase security aware-ness in the event the National Terrorism Advisory System (NTAS) issues an Imminent Threat Alert or Elevated Threat Alert. The heightened security alert procedure should also be used based on world conditions or information received by actual law enforcement intelligence of terrorist activities or other types of activities that could jeopardize the safety of employees, guests, visitors, and the property. Prior to implementing this procedure, a meeting should be conducted with the key leaders and decision-makers of the property—usually the executive team. The nature and type of alert or threat should be discussed and the actions taken should be agreed upon and implemented. There should also be predeter-mined follow-up meetings to discuss any updates pertaining to the threat or alert. This procedure is designed to phase-in as the perceived level of risk assessment increases. The heightened security procedures are as follows:

I. *Building Exterior Perimeter*
- The security surveillance center in addition to vehicles, bikes, and external patrols, will maintain a constant patrol of the perimeter of the building.
- Vehicles should be allowed to stop or park along the curb line adja-cent to the building.
- Delivery trucks should be stopped to examine the delivery bill of lading prior to entry into the building and/or dock areas.
- Perimeter patrols should ensure all emergency exits remain closed and secure.

II. *Valet/Special Parking Areas*
- Signs should be posted indicating that the insides of vehicles, trunks, and cargo areas are subject to inspection before vehicles will be accepted for valet or special parking areas.
- The security surveillance center will patrol key areas using the CCTV system, and personnel will be positioned at key areas such as in valet areas or in the designated vehicle drop-off areas to con-duct inspections of those vehicles dropping people off or being parked in these areas.
- Any person arriving who does not wish their vehicle to be inspected will be requested to park off site.

Valet/Special Parking Sign Example:

Attention: Valet and Special Parking Areas

For your safety and security, all vehicles are subject to a visual security inspection of the interior, trunk, and/or cargo areas prior to using the valet or special parking areas. Those not willing to have the inspection take place, please utilize off-site parking areas.

III. *Building Interior Perimeter*
   • The security surveillance center will patrol the area using the CCTV system, and personnel will establish a back-of-house perimeter patrol to screen for unauthorized persons.
   • Credentials will be verified, and employee status of anyone in the back-of-house areas who is not displaying the proper credentials will be confirmed.

IV. *Loading Docks (After Normal Operating Hours)*
   The security surveillance center will patrol the area using the CCTV system, and personnel will be assigned to patrol the loading dock after hours when the dock is not normally in use to prevent unauthorized access.

V. *Entrance Control*
   Depending on the type of threat and suspected activity, the security surveillance center will patrol the area using the CCTV system and personnel will be assigned to patrol the entrances to ensure no large bags, backpacks, briefcases, etc., are permitted on premises.

VI. *Controlling Property Access Roads*
   For an extra layer of protection, the security surveillance center will patrol the area using the CCTV system, and personnel will be assigned to posts and conduct patrols of the main access roads leading into the property from public roadways. Visual inspections are to be conducted, and all unusual or suspicious activity is to be immediately reported to the security surveillance center leadership team.

The following is an example of the implementation of these procedures. These are general guidelines and, if necessary, should be modified to meet the specific individual needs of your property.

1. Intelligence information is received from law enforcement that warns of a credible threat.

Implement Sections I, II, and III.

2. Intelligence information is received from law enforcement that indicates that there is a credible, specific, and impending threat.

Implement Sections I, II, III, IV, V, and VI.

STANDARD OPERATING PROCEDURE: 000

Fire Emergency

Effective Date:
Revision Date:
Approval:

Since many fire command centers are located in the security surveillance center, the following is a general process and procedure designed to cover the basics for a variety of jurisdictions. Consult with and refer to your local jurisdictional representative for the specific requirements and responsibilities for your area.

RESPONSE PROCEDURES FOR FIRE EMERGENCY

The reasons the fire department must be contacted include the following:

- The fire alarm system has been automatically or manually activated.
- The fire is in the free burning or open-flame stage.
- A portable fire extinguisher has been utilized to control a fire.

Fire Alarm Print-out

- Any fire-related alarm received by the security surveillance center via the fire alarm computer system is automatically printed out with the following information:
  - Type of alarm (fire, supervisory, room director, system trouble)
  - Zone number and location of alarm
  - Time and date of alarm
- Types of alarms:
  - *Priority one* (fire): Sets off horns and strobes and will recall elevators and close alarm actuated doors. Immediate response is required, and appropriate personnel are to be notified and dispatched to the alarm location.
  - *Priority two*: Includes supervisory alarms, room detectors, and trouble alarms. Will not set off horns or strobes or recall elevators or close alarm actuated doors. Appropriate personnel are to be notified and dispatched to the alarm location.

RESPONSE PROCEDURES FOR FIRE EMERGENCY (Alarm)

Priority 1 (Pull Station, Water Flow, Smoke Detector)

- Alarm received and acknowledged on the fire panel located in the security surveillance center. The system is not to be restored until after the alarm malfunction has been identified by the leadership of the appropriate responding departments—security, facilities, and fire department.

- Security surveillance center personnel use CCTV to bring up camera views of the area of the reported alarm.
- Notification of:
  - Fire department via 911
  - Emergency services (if needed)
  - Appropriate property departments
- After ensuring that it is safe to do so, security surveillance center personnel will dispatch the appropriate personnel to the scene of the alarm. Personnel dispatched to the scene will maintain radio contact with the security surveillance center and provide updates and information pertaining to the conditions.
- The security surveillance center confirms that a representative of the security leadership team is reporting/has arrived to the security surveillance center to meet with the fire department and provide an escort to the location of the alarm.
- Voice communications are activated (if necessary) by security surveillance center personnel to alert patrons/employees of the situation.
- The date, time, and any comments will be documented by a member of the security surveillance center after the "all clear" is given by the fire department.

Trouble Signals (Power Failure, Ground Fault, Pump Failure)

- Alarm received and acknowledged in the security surveillance center.

Supervisory Alarms (Fire Pump Running, Tamper Switch, Low Air Pressure)

- Alarm received and acknowledged in the security surveillance center.
- Security surveillance center personnel notifies the maintenance department and documents activity.
- If the system is restored immediately, security surveillance center personnel will record and document.

System Testing, Construction, or Fire Watch

- Maintenance notifies the security surveillance center of areas to be tested. The security surveillance center will notify the fire department.
- Security surveillance center personnel record and document the information.

A fire watch is required when the fire protection system will be out of service for more than 4 hours in a 24-hour period. A fire watch will be provided for all areas that are left unprotected. The fire watch will remain in effect until the fire protection system is returned to service. The duties of personnel performing a fire watch detail include the following:

- In multiple-story facilities, one member of the fire watch team is to be assigned to every three floors.

- Patrol of the entire facility should be completed every 30 minutes. The exemption to this is if the facility has people sleeping in it, has institutional occupancy, or has assembly occupancy. In these cases, the entire facility should be patrolled every 15 minutes.
- Maintain a log of fire watch activities. This log should be available to the fire department at all times during the fire watch. The log should include the following:
  - Address of facility
  - Name of person conducting fire watch
  - Time that patrol has completed each tour of the facility
  - Record of any communications to the fire department or monitoring company
- Any gaps in coverage will be documented by the security surveillance center and immediately corrected.
- Personnel assigned to the fire watch detail must maintain radio communications with the security surveillance center.
- Personnel assigned to fire watch must have specific knowledge of exactly which warning devices are out of service.
- Personnel assigned to fire watch must know the proper evacuation route in the event of an emergency situation.
- Personnel assigned to fire watch must have knowledge of the location and use of fire extinguishers.

Security surveillance center personnel will notify the fire department and monitoring company when the fire protection system has been fully resorted. Security surveillance center personnel will document the person, date, and time the notification was made.

STANDARD OPERATING PROCEDURE: 000

Impairment of Life Safety Systems

Effective Date:
Revision Date:
Approval:

To ensure the safety of guests, visitors, and employees, the impairment notification form must be legibly completed and signed anytime the fire control system is serviced, tested, or any part of the system is placed into the bypass mode. The impairment notification should include the following:

- Date of request
- Time of request
- Company/Person making request

- Emergency contact number
- Type of impairment
- Systems to be taken for service
- Duration of impairment
- Reason for impairment
- Date placed back in service
- Time placed back in service
- Who placed system back in service

An entry must be made into the daily activity report indicating the date, time, and pertinent information regarding the impairment notification.

The impairment notification form is kept and maintained in the security surveillance center. Upon completion of service, test, or bypass, the impairment notification form must be immediately updated by the person or company that initially made the impairment notification. An entry must be made into the daily activity report indicating the date, time, and pertinent information regarding the restoration of the system.

5 Fire Command

This chapter is designated for security surveillance centers that operate the fire command center for the property. The evolution of the fire command center being located in this area increases the ability for confirmation of an alert on the fire panel, to be instantaneous, as being an actual event or an alarm malfunction. In the past, and at properties where the fire alarm panel location is not associated with the security surveillance center, the response to an activation on the panel can be very disjointed.

Think about this for a minute. For properties that do not have their fire command center located in the same area as the security surveillance center, a responder has to go to the panel and identify the location. The location where the CCTV system is located is contacted via radio or telephone and verbally advised of the event and location. The CCTV operator must then confirm the location and attempt to locate the event. This takes time and, unfortunately, in a worst-case scenario a few seconds or even minutes can be the difference between a quick response, identification of the issue, and dispatching appropriate emergency personnel, or a catastrophic event.

On the other hand, when the Fire Control Center (FCC) is located within the framework of the security surveillance center, all of the needed information is gathered instantly as the fire panel alert is transmitted. This saves time, which results in a quick, efficient, and effective response regarding the identification of the alarm. This, in turn, provides safety and protection to the company assets, guest, and employees.

When the fire command center is intertwined with the security surveillance center, the security surveillance center personnel should be familiar with the basic operations and components of the fire alarm system. The following are the basic operations of fire alarm systems that report to the security surveillance center via the FCC.

- *Manual fire alarm*: Includes pull stations—when the bar is pulled, it activates audiovisual devices. This is a type 1 alarm—when activated, it automatically activates horns, strobes, speakers, and so on. The area of alarm must be physically inspected and cleared prior to the resetting of this alarm type.
- *Automatic fire detection*: Includes smoke and heat detectors.
- *Intelligent or addressable analog fire detectors*: Microprocessors and microcomputer-controlled panel and devices.
- *Voice alarm and activation*: A public address system that communicates information by a human voice providing instruction to evacuating a structure or status of an alarm condition.
- *Sprinklers and fire suppression systems*: Interfaced with the fire alarm system to automatically recall elevators and activate sprinklers.
- *Building controls*: Designed to interface with various systems that control electrical and mechanical systems within a building. These include electrical lights, backup power, fire pumps, water pumps, air control, and vent control.

The following are the basic components of fire alarm systems that report to the security surveillance center via the FCC:

- *Control panel*: This is the brains of the system—it processes the information from the field devices, such as pull stations, and triggers the audiovisual devices when it determines that an alarm condition is present. It also monitors and supervises the integrity of the power supply.
- *Standby power supply*: In the event of a power outage, the standby power supply would keep the system operational for a predetermined amount of time. The standby power supply usually consists of batteries charged with a battery charger or is engine powered with the generator being fueled by gas or diesel.
- *Annunciator status panel*: Identifies the condition status of an alarm, alarm type, or location of trouble of fault. An indicator light flashes on the panel identifying the location of the zone in alarm. Depending on the type of alarm, responders can control the alarm system by using a reset switch or code to silence the alarm or reset the system.
- *Field devices*: Devices used in the initiating zone including heat detectors, smoke detectors, pull station, and audiovisual devices.

There are two basic types of fire alarm systems used in security surveillance centers:

- *Single-stage system*: When a device is activated, it is designed to immediately transmit an alarm signal throughout the entire facility to warn occupants that a fire emergency exists. For example, in most jurisdictions, a pull station is categorized as a single-stage device.
- *Two-stage system*: This system is designed to transmit a distinct alert signal to security surveillance center personnel. The source of the alarm is to be investigated immediately. If a fire condition is present, they are to actuate the signal. There is a predetermined period of time in which an alarm signal is automatically activated if the proper personnel do not activate or reset the alarm system. Two-stage alarm systems are used to reduce the possibility of risk and injury when evacuating a facility due to an alarm malfunction that could result in jeopardizing the safety of the occupants due to a nonevent. It is essential that security surveillance center personnel be instructed in the proper procedures to follow before silencing an alarm. In most jurisdictions, the activation of two smoke sensors would activate the single-stage system.

The following are the four basic stages of fire:

- *First stage—incipient stage*: During the first incipient stage, which could last for seconds to days, there is no noticeable smoke, heat, or flame. Infrared (IR) and ultraviolet (UV) radiant energy is the earliest signature from a fire. During this stage, flammable gases and/or combustion products are emitted. This is the earliest stage of a fire.

- *Second stage—smoldering stage*: There is still no substantial amount of flame or heat, but there is enough combustion to create visible smoke.
- *Third stage*: The flame stage usually involves less smoke, but flames break out and generate substantial heat.
- *Fourth stage*: Often referred to as the high-heat stage, fire spreads rapidly producing extensive flames, extreme heat, and many toxic gases.

Oxygen, heat, and fuel are the three basic elements needed for a fire. These three elements are also known as the fire triangle. When one of these elements is removed, it will cause a side of the triangle to be broken and the fire will die. Fire extinguishers and fire extinguisher systems are important components in eliminating one or more sides of the fire triangle.

Fire is classified into the following: Class A, Class B, Class C, and Class D, and Class K:

- *Class A*: Consist of fire that involves wood, cloth, paper, rubber, or other carbonaceous solids. Water is used to quench the fire and cool the material below its ignition temperature.
- *Class B*: Consist of fire involving flammable or combustible liquids, gases, and greases. This includes gasoline, oil, and paint. Dry powder, foam, carbon dioxide, or vaporizing liquid interrupts and smothers the fuel oxygen of the heat triangle.
- *Class C*: Usually involves a Class A or Class B fire and also involves energized electrical equipment. A nonenergized agent is critical. When the agent melts, it forms an oxygen coating over the burning material to suffocate them. Carbon dioxide, dry powder, or vaporizing liquid is effective. Since water and foam are conductive, they should not be used.
- *Class D*: Usually involves certain combustible metals such as magnesium, sodium, potassium, and their alloys. A special dry powder that has a special smothering and coating agent should be used. This agent is not suited for use on other classes of fires.
- *Class K*: Usually involves cooking oils and greases such as animal and vegetable fats. Saponification is the fastest and most effective way to fight this type of fire. Fire extinguishers rated for this type of fire contain a wet chemical agent that turns the cooking oil and fat that is serving as fuel into soap.

It is important to be familiar with the proper way to combat each of the classes of fire. An agent that works perfectly on one class of fire can have disastrous results on another. The acronym PASS has helped me remember the proper way to use a fire extinguisher:

P—Pull the pin of the fire extinguisher (located at the top by the handle).
A—Aim the fire extinguisher at the base of the fire.
S—Squeeze the handle of the fire extinguisher.
S—Sweep the fire extinguisher from side to side at the base of the fire.

Because of the electronic equipment located inside of the security surveillance center, the following gas suppression systems are good choices for fire suppression.

- The Aero-K system uses an aerosol of microscopic potassium compounds, which it releases from small canisters mounted on walls near the ceiling. These Aero-K generators are not pressurized until fire is detected. The Aero-K system uses multiple fire detectors in a two-stage system and does not release until a fire is "confirmed" by two or more detectors. The gas is noncorrosive and is not harmful to security surveillance center equipment such as metals, electrical equipment, or media.
- The FM-200 system is a colorless, liquefied compressed gas. It is stored as a liquid and dispenses as a colorless, nonconductive vapor that is clear and does not obscure vision. It leaves no residue and does not displace oxygen.

When writing this chapter regarding the fire command component of the security surveillance center, I struggled with the best way to present this material. I wanted this section to be useful, uncomplicated, and easy to understand. I also did not want these policies to be simply copied and used. The reason for this is that the rules, regulations, codes, and laws governing the areas enveloped under the fire command umbrella of the security surveillance center has the possibility of being different in every jurisdiction. As you will see, I have decided to include the general process and procedures.

Keep in mind that these are designed to cover the basics for a variety of jurisdictions. These are to be used simply as a guide and are designed to provide a starting point for your procedures regarding the fire command component of the security surveillance center. It is very important to review and understand the equipment being utilized, how it operates, and the rules, regulations, codes, and laws that govern this area of your facility. Consult with, meet, and develop a great rapport with your local jurisdictional representatives responsible for this area and follow the facility's established protocol, policy, and procedures regarding the specific requirements and responsibilities for your location.

The goal of standard operating procedures is to establish communications between the entities involved in fire management and fire evacuation operations to limit the loss of life and property from the effects of fire and provide first aid at the scene and rescue persons during an emergency. Mutual assistance and prior coordination with the fire department are critical. For this reason, it is important to review the standard operating procedures pertaining to this area with the leader or liaison of the local fire department. Make sure that the fire department has a copy of your fire and disaster plan and procedure. Develop a rapport with the representative and invite the representative to participate in your exercises and training programs. Also ask if the facility can participate in the fire department's training exercises. When it comes to life and safety, there can never be too much communication, and the interaction between all departments regarding this area should be encouraged.

STANDARD OPERATING PROCEDURE: 000

Fire Command

Effective Date:

Revision Date:

Approval:

Fire Alarm Printout

1. Any fire-related alarm received by the security surveillance center via the fire alarm computer system is automatically printed out with the following information:
   a. Type of alarm (fire, supervisory, room director, system trouble)
   b. Zone number and location of alarm
   c. Time and date of alarm
2. Types of alarms include the following:
   a. *Priority one* (fire): Sets off horns and strobes and will recall elevators and close alarm-actuated doors. Immediate response is required as per standard operating procedures.
   b. *Priority two*: Includes supervisory alarms and trouble alarms. Will not set off horns or strobes or recall elevators or close alarm-actuated doors.
   c. *Alarm malfunctions*: When an alarm is activated and there is no sign of smoke or fire. If there is no sign of smoke or fire, an "all-clear notification" should be reported to the security surveillance center.

Note that all nonemergency radio traffic should cease until the alarm has been verified as being a malfunction or the situation has been resolved.

Priority 1 (Pull Station and Water Flow)

1. Alarm received and acknowledged on FCC panel in the security surveillance center. (Do not restore the system until after an alarm malfunction has been determined and verified by responding personnel.)
2. The security surveillance center operator brings up the camera view of the alarm location and area on the CCTV system.
3. Notification of the following:
   a. Fire department via 911 hotline
   b. Security Surveillance Personnel and Maintenance
   c. Appropriate departments
4. A second member of the security surveillance center who is not monitoring the fire system should dispatch appropriate personnel to the scene of the alarm, provided that it does not jeopardize safety. Personnel dispatched to scene will maintain radio contact with the security surveillance center and will report conditions and provide updates on the conditions at the alarm site.

5. The maintenance leader will dispatch appropriate personnel to the sight of the alarm.
6. Security surveillance center personnel should confirm that a representative of the security surveillance center leadership team is reporting or has arrived at the security surveillance center to meet with the fire department and provide an escort to the location of the event.
7. Voice communications are activated (if necessary) by security surveillance center personnel to alert patrons/employees of the situation.
8. Security surveillance center personnel verifies the fire department response.
9. Prior to arrival of the fire department, security surveillance center personnel will provide a brief description of the situation to a representative of the security surveillance center leadership team.
10. A representative of the security surveillance center leadership team will communicate information pertaining to the situation to the fire department battalion chief.
11. A representative of the security surveillance center leadership team will provide an escort for fire department personnel to the scene.
12. After "all-clear" notification is given by the fire department, comments will be recorded in the daily activity report by security surveillance center personnel.

Trouble Signals (Power Failure—Ground Fault)

• Alarm received and acknowledged in security surveillance center.

Supervisory Alarms (Tamper Switch—Low Air Pressure)

1. Alarm received and acknowledged in the security surveillance center.
2. Security surveillance center personnel notify the maintenance department.
3. If the system is restored immediately, a record is made in the daily activity report in the security surveillance center.

STANDARD OPERATING PROCEDURE: 000

Fire Watch

Effective Date:
Revision Date:
Approval:

In the event that a fire watch is to be implemented, the following procedures should be followed:

• The security surveillance center notifies the fire department.
• The security surveillance center notifies the monitoring company.
• The security surveillance operator records the information on a daily log.

The security surveillance center contacts a representative of the security surveillance center leadership team and advises of the situation.

- A representative of the security surveillance center leadership team will establish a fire watch detail containing one representative per three floors.
- The security surveillance center will report any gaps in coverage to a representative of the security surveillance center leadership team.
- The security surveillance center representative will have knowledge and location of the use of fire protection equipment such as fire extinguishers.
- The security representative will maintain a log of fire watch activities and be available to the fire department at all times during the fire watch.
- Fire watch personnel cannot have other duties besides their assigned fire watch. However, the fire department may designate other duties.
- Fire watch personnel will not perform firefighting duties beyond the scope of an ordinary citizen.
- Fire watch personnel should conduct fire watch patrols every 15 to 30 minutes.
- Fire watch personnel must maintain radio communications with the security surveillance center.
- A security surveillance center representative must have specific knowledge of which warning devices are out of service.
- A security surveillance center representative must know the proper evacuation route in the event of an emergency situation.
- The security surveillance center should maintain a fire watch log available to the fire department at all times during the fire watch.
- The fire watch log should contain the following:
  - Address of facility
  - Time that the fire watch patrol has been completed for each fire watch tour of the facility
  - Name of the person conducting the fire watch
  - Record of the communication(s) to fire department and monitoring company
  - Record of other information as requested by fire department personnel
- When the fire watch is completed, a member of the security surveillance center will notify and record the communications of the cancellation of the fire watch to the fire department and monitoring company in the daily activity report.

In the event that an actual fire watch is implemented, the following is a guide that should be utilized and distributed to those involved and participating in the event.

FIRE WATCH

- A fire watch is the action of an on-site person whose sole responsibility is to watch for the occurrence of fire.

FIRE WATCH REQUIREMENTS

- When a required fire protection system is out of service for more than 4 hours in a 24-hour period, the authority having jurisdiction will be notified, and the building will be evacuated *or* an approved fire watch will be implemented for all areas left unprotected until the fire protection system has been returned to service.
- A fire watch should involve some special action beyond normal staffing; additional personnel who are specially trained in fire prevention should be assigned to patrol the affected areas.

FIRE WATCH DUTIES

- Periodic patrols of the affected areas and facility should be conducted.
- Direct communication with the fire department (i.e., telephone) is necessary.
- Identify any life, fire, or property hazards.
- If an emergency situation is discovered, notify 911 with the exact address and type of emergency.
- If the facility needs to be evacuated, notify the occupants.
- Maintain a log of fire watch activities.
- Have knowledge of location and use of fire protection equipment (i.e., fire extinguishers).
- Fire watch personnel cannot have other duties.
- Fire watch personnel will not perform firefighting duties beyond the scope of an ordinary citizen.

RECORDKEEPING

- A fire watch log should be maintained at the facility. The log must be available to the fire department at all times during the fire watch. The fire watch log should contain the following:
  - Address of facility, name of the person conducting the fire watch, times that each patrol was completed.
  - Communications to the fire department and monitoring company.
  - Any other information as directed by the fire department.

CANCELLATION OF FIRE WATCH

- Once the fire protection system has been fully restored, it is the responsibility of the facility to cancel the fire watch.
- Once the fire watch has been cancelled, it is the responsibility of the facility to make all of the proper notifications, including notification to the fire department and monitoring company.

STANDARD OPERATING PROCEDURE: 000

Fire and Evacuations

Effective Date:
Revision Date:
Approval:

In the event of a fire alarm or actual fire, it will be the security surveillance center's responsibility to ensure that policies are implemented and followed in order to protect lives and company assets. All employees are responsible for minimizing danger to the occupants of the property. Because the security surveillance center has the ability to obtain an overall view of different areas of the entire property and can quickly assess and communicate events in real time to the appropriate areas, the security surveillance center leadership team will be the primary source for coordinating emergency information. It will be the responsibility of the security surveillance center leadership team to ensure that all company policies and procedures are carried out and ensure that full cooperation is provided to the fire department, law enforcement, and other emergency responders. The fire department is the governing authority whenever their services are needed. Their instructions are to be explicitly followed.

In the event of an emergency, a member of the security surveillance center leadership team will designate a command post. This command post should have a telephone, table, chairs, and adequate space to accommodate key personnel.

ALARMS

When an alarm is activated, the security surveillance center personnel will observe the following protocol when active fire alarms are reported to the security surveillance center:

1. The location and type of alarm will register on the fire alarm control panel.
2. Security surveillance center personnel will be dispatched to the alarm site to investigate the alarm and determine if it is an actual fire. (In some jurisdictions, there is an allotment of 180 seconds to respond and determine if it is an actual event, before the fire department is notified.)
3. The fire department will be contacted by security surveillance center personnel.
4. Visuals (strobe lights) will be activated and an audio (horn and public announcement systems) announcement to evacuate will occur.
5. A member of the leadership team of the security surveillance center will assign personnel to report to the designated fire lane, clear the fire lane of all bystanders and vehicle obstructions, and await the arrival of the fire department.

FIRE

When personnel discover a fire or evidence of a fire, it will be immediately broadcast as an alert message over the radio or telephone to the security surveillance center.

The radio transmission must include the *exact location*, nature, and disposition of the fire.

The following are the operational responses for the security surveillance center personnel to take upon receipt of an alert message, reported fire, or confirmed fire event:

1. The fire department will be notified immediately by security surveillance center personnel.
2. Personnel will be dispatched to the scene to assist in extinguishing the fire.
3. A member of the leadership team of the security surveillance center will assemble a command post and await the arrival of the fire department.

All members of the security surveillance center should be familiar with the overall layout and physical aspects of the facility. A thorough knowledge of the property is important to expedite the handling of emergency situations. Security surveillance center personnel awareness will serve to effectively, efficiently, and professionally combat potentially dangerous situations. Remember that other than a fire and a fire alarm itself, panic poses a serious threat of danger. It is the responsibility of security surveillance center personnel to maintain a calm, professional demeanor when dealing with any emergency situation. It is important to establish an attitude of reassurance when communicating and dealing with an event. This helps induce a general calming effect upon others.

EVACUATIONS

The evacuation program is a guide for the safe, efficient movement of occupants out of various areas of the property in order to protect and preserve human life, while at the same time minimizing loss to the company. General areas should be treated individually, but preliminary procedures will remain the same. From time to time, on-the-spot adjustments of procedures, to protect lives, may have to be made.

AUTHORITY TO ORDER AN EVACUATION

Upon receipt of a general (priority one) alarm, the systems audio and visual devices will activate automatically and after an investigative phase takes place, a member of the security surveillance center will make an announcement to evacuate the building.

In the event of a confirmed fire or other life-threatening situation, it will be the responsibility of a member of the security surveillance center team to make appropriate notifications and review the CCTV system to ensure that appropriate action is being taken and that occupants of the facility are moved to safety.

NOTIFICATION PROCEDURES

Each department leader notified will have the responsibility of notifying the appropriate personnel within their department. The leader of the security surveillance center, or designee, will immediately notify the president of the property. When the order to evacuate is received, each department will implement its departmental evacuation procedures. (The following is a list of various departments and evacuation roles and responsibilities for each. Remember that these are examples and should be modified to meet your properties specific needs.)

PBX DEPARTMENT

1. Coordinate all telephone communications during the emergency. Incoming should be prioritized in the following manner:
   a. Security surveillance center extensions
   b. Extensions in affected area
   c. In-house telephones
   d. Outside calls

Personnel will leave their work areas in a calm and orderly fashion.

MAINTENANCE

The maintenance department will be responsible for making sure that immediate access is available to any affected area at the request of the security surveillance center. Additionally, maintenance will be placed on alert and be ready to immediately shut down power to any area.

BEVERAGE AREAS

Bar area personnel will close and lock any cabinets containing bottles of liquor. Bartenders will close and lock all registers and will turn the key over to a member of the beverage leadership team. A member of the beverage leadership team from each bar will make certain that all registers are locked and then maintain the keys until they are turned over to a security surveillance center leader.

Beverage servers will leave their work areas in a calm and orderly fashion.

FOOD AREAS

Food servers will leave their work areas in a calm and orderly fashion.

Operators of equipment will turn off all equipment and other machinery in their work stations and leave in a calm and orderly fashion.

Chefs will turn off all ranges, grills, ovens, etc., and will calmly leave the area.

Provided it is safe to do so, the leader of the area will conduct a check of the area to ensure all have departed and that the previously listed tasks were completed.

CASHIERS

Cashiers will close and lock their registers and turn the key over to a member of their leadership team. If possible, and if safe to do so, this should be done prior to leaving the building.

Cashiers will leave their work areas in a calm and orderly fashion.

WINDOWS AND DOORS

In the event of a fire, all windows and doors will be kept closed as much as possible to prevent ventilation. Doors between stairways and floors will be kept closed to prevent drafts.

SECURITY SURVEILLANCE CENTER ASSIGNMENTS

During all evacuation procedures, security surveillance center personnel will review areas to make certain that occupants are out of the building. Personnel who are in the field should respond to the back of the house employee areas to assist in the evacuation of employees and to prevent access back into the employee areas until the emergency is cleared. Employees should be directed to the staging area. Reiterate the message for employees to leave the area via the nearest emergency exit until the emergency is cleared.

Once all personnel have cleared the area, no one will be permitted back inside except by the direction of the fire department. Only after the fire department give the "all-clear notification" to the leadership of the property will anyone be permitted to return to the cleared areas.

STANDARD OPERATING PROCEDURE: 000

Impairment of Life Safety Systems

Effective Date:
Revision Date:
Approval:

To ensure the safety of guests, visitors, and employees, the impairment notification form must be legibly completed and signed anytime the fire control system is serviced or tested, or any part of the system is placed into the bypass mode. An entry must be made into the daily activity report indicating the date, time, and pertinent information regarding the impairment notification.

The impairment notification form is kept and maintained in the security surveillance center. Upon completion of service, test, or bypass, the impairment notification form must be immediately updated by the person(s) or company who initially made the impairment notification. An entry must be made into the daily activity report indicating the date, time, and pertinent information regarding the restoration of the system.

The impairment notification form should include the following:

- Date of request
- Time of request
- Company/Person making request
- Emergency contact phone number
- Type of impairment
- Systems to be taken for service
- Duration of impairment
- Reason for impairment
- Date placed back into service
- Time placed back into service
- Who placed system back into service

6 Legal Perspectives, Ethics, and the Fourth Amendment

I have decided to place ethics and legal perspectives together since these two topics tend to go hand in hand. If poor ethical decisions are made, they will eventually lead situations into the legal arena. This chapter examines the security surveillance center from a legal and ethical perspective and the important role these perspectives play in the operation and perception of the security surveillance center.

The following is an incident that I was involved in while patrolling the New Jersey Turnpike. On August 22, 1989, while performing my duties as a New Jersey State Trooper, during a motor vehicle stop I was shot six times. God was on my side that day and, after much rehabilitation, I was able to return to society and lead an active and productive life. When I was on the mend, my fellow troopers held a surprise dinner for me and over 200 troopers, dignitaries, the governor, and past and current colonels of the New Jersey State Police attended. To say the least, it was an honor and privilege to be recognized by my fellow comrades. Among the items presented to me was a quote based upon the address delivered at Sorbonne, Paris, on April 23, 1910, by Theodore Roosevelt, "Dare To Do." It was framed, handwritten in calligraphy, and read aloud by the presenter. As it was being read, I noticed a former lieutenant of mine, whom I respected very much, knew the words by heart and was reading along. I have always treasured the memory of the support and kindness demonstrated to me on that day by so many.

Ever since that day, I have placed this gift on the wall in my office of every place I have ever worked. I have used this as a springboard by reviewing with others and bringing up the topic of ethics and discussing the meaning of the words in the address. I enjoy hearing what they mean to the person who reads them for the first time and describing to them what it means to me. I have handed out copies and reviewed this with many members of the teams I have had the opportunity to be part of.

DARE TO DO

It is not the critic who counts, not the man who points out how the strong man stumbled, or where the doer of deeds could have done them better. The credit belongs to the man who is actually in the arena; whose face is marred by dust and sweat and blood; who strives valiantly, who errs and comes short again and again, because there is no effort without error and shortcoming; who does actually strive to do the deeds, who knows the great enthusiasms, the great devotions, spends himself in a worthy cause; who at the best knows in the end the triumph of achievement, and who at the worst, if he fails, at least he fails while daring greatly, so that his place shall never be with those cold and timid souls who know neither victory nor defeat.

T. Roosevelt

WHAT IS ETHICS?

Some people say that ethics is what somebody does when no one is watching them. Theodore Roosevelt said that "to educate a man in mind, but not in morals is to create a menace to society." It is for this reason that the topic of ethics is such a vital component of anyone who views themselves as a professional. Security surveillance center personnel must do technical things correctly, and they also must do ethically correct things. Everyone encounters ethical dilemmas, and for these reasons it is important for security surveillance personnel to know, understand, and demonstrate a high degree of ethics, morals, and values. The hope is that a person makes the right decision, and if not, understands why. To aid in the understanding of this area, the following is a brief synopsis of ethics, morals, and values.

Ethics is moral standards and how they affect conduct. The Greek root for *ethics* is "ethos," which stresses the perfection of the individual and the community that the individual belongs to. There are many aspects of ethics. Ethics is about what is right and what is wrong; it is about vice and virtue. Ethics is about benefit and harm. Ethics describes what should be. Ethics is the way morals are practiced.

Morality originates from the Latin word *moralis,* which means "traditional customs or proper behavior." Basically, morals refer to a set of rules defining what is considered to be right or wrong and accepted by everyone in a group or society. If someone breaks such a rule, that person is typically considered to be immoral. Morals are values that an individual attributes to a system of beliefs that assists the individual in defining right from wrong or good from bad. Charles Colson makes a clear and concise synopsis of the difference between morals and ethics. He stated, "Morality describes what is. Ethics describes what ought to be."

Values provide direction in determining right from wrong or good from bad. Values are what a person believes to be valuable, to have worth or importance. Ethics, morals, and values all seem to be interconnected with one another in one way or another.

ETHICS IN PRACTICE

Knowing only the definitions of ethics, morals, and values is not enough to ensure that they will be practiced. Critical thinking must be applied and demonstrated by consciously using reason to make the best decision. Alternately, acting on impulse or in a repetitive manner is not acceptable, especially when dealing with matters of ethical concern or the well-being of others.

Ethics begins with the person. A company or department cannot have ethics; it is its employees who have ethics. It is the leadership team that makes ethical decisions. I believe, for the most part, the majority of people desire to be ethical, most companies desire to act ethically, and everyone desires to be treated ethically. The difficult part is to communicate and calibrate the thinking of individuals and an organization's shared values and their process of decision-making. The first step, for the purpose of ethics, is to make individuals morally better, respect other's rights, fulfill obligations, treat others fairly, and be truthful in both words and actions.

Ethical decision-making and implementation require both critical thinking and communication skills. For our purposes, I am going to outline the three basic steps involved in this process: personal morality, professional ethics, and organizational ethics.

1. Personal morality, or an individual's concept of right and wrong, is developed based on upbringing and environment.
2. Professional ethics is typically codified within an organization as it relates to the organization or position.
3. Organizational ethics are the written policies and procedures that lay out the company's expectations relating to ethical decision-making and behavior.

Many times, ethics and professionalism go hand in hand. What is professionalism? The *American College Dictionary* defines the root word of professionalism in the following manner:

A profession is a "vocation *requiring* knowledge of some department of learning of science."

A professional is one who follows "an occupation as a means of livelihood or gain," or one who is "engaged in one of the *learned* professions."

Professionalism is exhibited by one of the "professional character, spirit, or methods" or the "standing, practice, or methods of a professional as *distinguished from an amateur*."

Professionalism has many meanings depending on the environment that it is being used. There are many factors that people use to base their opinion on whether someone is professional. Some of the areas include the manner in which someone dresses, performs, reacts under pressure, and communicates, both verbally and nonverbally. A person's appearance, actions, and communication style during the day-to-day operation with others should display a sense of confidence as it has an impact on determining if a person, department, or organization is professional.

Professionals generally exhibit a behavior that is focused, accountable, confident, competent, goal oriented, respectful, and conveys a sense of urgency. Security surveillance center professionals should not react emotionally when handling stressful situations. Critical situations should be handled in a serious, effective, and efficient manner. There is a time and a place for humor—when used well it has a relieving effect, when used improperly it can be disastrous. Over the course of time and experiences, the security surveillance center professional will develop a sense of when humor is appropriate to alleviate a situation, and when it is not.

Some of the major elements of professionalism are a code of ethics, philosophy, knowledge, guidelines, and standardization of job performance. The code of ethics plays a key role in developing synergy and integrating the other key components that help establish professionalism in a security surveillance center. At times in my career there were occasions when I reported to leaders who chose to operate in the marginal areas when it came to behaving and conducting business in an ethical manner. When this type of scenario presents itself, it is best to address the situation. Being the eternal optimist, the hope is that the behavior of the individual will change, and the person will be thankful that this was brought to his or her attention.

However, unfortunately sometimes leadership may not want to know that there is a thousand pound elephant in the room and elect not to address questionable ethical behavior by members of its key leadership team. If this should happen, as I have found myself in the past, the best advice that I can give is to pack your bags and work someplace else. The most important things that a security surveillance center professional has in his or her tool chest are character, morals, and ethics. These are the backbone of the components that separate the wheat from the chaff. As one of my great leaders in the past told me, "Ethics is what a person does when no one is watching." If a person cannot be trusted when people are watching, how is anyone expected to have confidence in him or her when that person is on his or her own. For these reasons, it is very important that a code of ethics be established, communicated, and adhered to by all levels of an organization. The following is a sample of a code of ethics that security surveillance centers should consider implementing to achieve a higher level of professionalism.

CODE OF ETHICS

- Security surveillance center personnel should, at all times, demonstrate a commitment to professionalism and diligence in the performance of duties.
- Security surveillance center personnel should not engage in any illegal or unethical conduct, or any activity that would constitute a conflict of interest.
- Security surveillance center personnel should, at all times, exhibit a high level of integrity in the performance of their duties.
- Security surveillance center personnel should comply with lawful orders of the courts and testify truthfully without bias or prejudice.
- Security surveillance center personnel, in reviewing coverage of an incident, investigations, and all other matters, should gather evidence or other documentation in a manner that establishes the facts.
- Security surveillance center personnel should not reveal any confidential information obtained during an investigation or an assignment without proper authorization.
- Security surveillance center personnel should present all material matters uncovered during the course of an investigation, review, or other matters, that if omitted, could cause a distortion of facts.
- Security surveillance center personnel should not focus on the position or status of persons involved in an investigation, review, or assignment.

- Security surveillance center personnel should continually strive for perfection by increasing their professional knowledge, competence, and effectiveness in all duties assigned or performed.
- Security surveillance center personnel should train and mentor others.

LEGAL PERSPECTIVES

The following pertains to the impact of the Fourth Amendment on security surveillance centers. The Fourth Amendment of the United States Constitution states, "the right of the people to be secure in their persons, houses, papers and effects, against unreasonable search and seizures, shall not be violated, and no Warrants shall issue, but upon probable cause, supported by an Oath or affirmation, and particularly describing the place to be searched, and the persons or things to be seized."

In the opinion of many scholars, when video surveillance of public areas is continuous, it generally does not present significant legalities. Interpretations of the Fourth Amendment as it pertains to video surveillance appear to be in favor of the use of closed-circuit television (CCTV) to protect the public. The belief is that continuous video surveillance does not intrude on an individual's sphere of privacy. It simply records events occurring in public space for which individuals do not have reasonable expectations of privacy.

SECURITY SURVEILLANCE CENTERS AND
FOURTH AMENDMENT IMPLICATIONS

Transactions in plain view in a public area generally do not raise Fourth Amendment concerns. This is known as the plain view rule and open-field doctrine. Current trends in interpreting and applying the Fourth Amendment do not classify this situation as a person, house, paper, or effects that are protected. The current opinion is that people videotaped in a public area have no reasonable expectations of privacy; therefore, it does not violate the Fourth Amendment.

The following provides support for permitting CCTV in public areas and roadways. The US Supreme Court in *Katz v. United States* 389 U.S. 347 (1967), defined modern search and seizure law under the Fourth Amendment. The court declared that "What a person knowingly exposes to the public, even in his own home or office, is not a subject of Fourth Amendment protection, but what he seeks to preserve as private, even in an area accessible to the public, may be constitutionally protected. Generally, a person walking along a public sidewalk or standing in a public park cannot reasonably expect that his activity will be immune from the public eye or from observation by the police."

Supreme Court in *United States v. Knotts 368 U.S. 276, 281–82 (1983)*

A person traveling in an automobile on public thoroughfares has no reasonable expectation of privacy in movements from one place to another. When [an individual] traveled over the public streets he voluntarily conveyed to anyone who wanted to look the fact that he was traveling over particular roads in a particular direction, and the fact of his final destination when he exited from public roads onto private property.

Conversely, CCTV observations occurring within an individual's house, or areas where there is an expectation of privacy, may violate the Fourth Amendment. One real-life example of this type of situation occurred when I was testing and auditing the CCTV of a security surveillance center of a property that I was opening on the east coast that was adjacent to condominiums. The security surveillance center had the ability to view into the condominiums. To ensure that the Fourth Amendment rights of those who lived in this area were not violated, I implemented measures that prevented the view of this area by the security surveillance center personnel. It is important to remember to check the ability of the cameras to view areas that are adjacent to public housing, including the pan–tilt–zoom (PTZ) feature. There is an expectation of privacy of those who live in residences that are on the border of businesses that have CCTV systems or security surveillance centers. Security surveillance centers should not use their CCTV systems to look into residences or it could be considered to be a violation of the Fourth Amendment.

The following article demonstrates and adds insight into various legal perspectives and the ethical considerations of incidents that could have an impact on security surveillance centers.

According to the *BBC News* article, "Assembly CCTV turn on homes":

> Security Guards of the assembly building in Cardiff Bay, United Kingdom were caught turning CCTV cameras onto nearby homes and hotels. Five employees received "significant" disciplinary penalties for the misuse. A spokesperson for the assembly said legal and police advice was taken as to whether a criminal investigation was appropriate. On their advice a decision was taken not to prosecute.

The Freedom of Information response read as follows:

> During the period stated in the request, five staff received disciplinary penalties for misusing CCTV equipment. Penalties were applied for the occasional misuse or suspected misuse of equipment by turning the cameras towards private dwellings therefore failing to focus on the security of the estate. Formal warnings were issued in all cases together with sanctions including amendments to terms and conditions and exclusion from promotion opportunities.... The disciplinary matters related to misuse of assembly equipment. The incidents of CCTV cameras being pointed towards private dwellings were isolated occurrences and there is no evidence to suggest that offenses were widespread in terms of frequency or practice. There has been no evidence of similar incidents since. Regular checks of the use of cameras are undertaken by management and action was taken quickly when these matters were discovered.

Why do people commit crime? One theory that attempts to explain why people commit crime is known as the routine activity theory. This theory is based on the belief that three factors are needed for prohibited incidents to occur:

- A motivated offender
- A suitable target
- Absence of a capable guardian

Even though a pool of motivated offenders will probably always exist, the establishment of a proactive security surveillance center helps to minimize the potential of motivated offenders by giving the perception of an increased level of capable guardianship. The presence of CCTV systems assists in the perception of visible security measures and helps to harden target areas of properties. The use of and proper placement of camera systems that are utilized by the security surveillance center and a general awareness and perception that someone is watching the CCTV cameras acts as a workforce multiplier by instilling the belief to the public and employees that inappropriate behavior and actions will lead to a response from the security surveillance center.

When measures are taken and there is an awareness that the area has become a hardened target, it tends to lead to the displacement of crime from the hardened area to locations away from the facility. When this occurs, it does not mean that similar types of crime stop happening everywhere, it merely means that the crimes may continue to occur, but not at the facility or area that instituted measures to make it more difficult to commit an act without being detected. Displacement is a valuable theory for those who wish for crime not to occur on areas under their jurisdiction or authority.

Taking the routine activity theory into consideration, and the possible role it plays in prohibited and unwanted behavior, security surveillance center professionals should factor this into the foreseeability approach and the totality of circumstances approach. It is important that security surveillance center personnel understand the significant difference between foreseeability and totality of the circumstances approaches and the role each plays in court decisions. The following is a brief explanation of each of these approaches.

FORESEEABILITY APPROACH

The foreseeability approach is the belief that a person with ordinary intelligence should have foreseen the impact of an action or scenario that would have put himself or herself or others in peril. This is when an event occurs that a reasonable person of average intelligence should have foreseen that their negligent act would put others or themselves in danger. In the past, courts have determined whether criminality is foreseeable by applying a prior similar acts approach, in which a crime is not considered foreseeable unless a pattern of similar crimes has occurred at a specific site.

TOTALITY OF CIRCUMSTANCES APPROACH

Another interesting area to explore is the totality of the circumstances approach in which courts consider all criminal incidents occurring on a landowner's property and adjacent properties as well as other types of evidence such as the nature, location, condition, and architectural design of the property. The totality of the circumstances approach places the burden of increasing security surveillance center measures on the property owners. It is pertinent that security surveillance center professionals implement security and safety measures that are indicative of illustrating that the company is supportive in proactively reviewing and, if necessary, revising any procedures, processes, or best practices to demonstrate a commitment to safety and security.

Since there is a significant difference between the foreseeability and totality of the circumstances approaches, it behooves all security surveillance center professionals to fully understand in which direction the pendulum of recent court decisions is swinging and trending in their areas of jurisdiction and implement security surveillance center measures accordingly. Best practices for security surveillance center professionals, regardless of jurisdiction and current trending of court decisions, is to consistently review the criminal statistics of the area, regularly analyze the property's security surveillance needs and incidents. The establishment of periodically reviewing a written security surveillance center plan involving law enforcement, tenants, civil leaders, and company leaders is always wise and beneficial to all. These practices could be invaluable in the event that a company is ever in the unenviable position of having to demonstrate that everything was done to prevent an incident from occurring.

The following articles are an insight into various legal perspectives and the ethical considerations of incidents that could have an impact on security surveillance centers. To avoid embarrassment, where possible, any specific company names or the names of individuals have been removed. The important lessons learned from the behaviors practiced are not impacted by these modifications.

According to the article, "Man Sues after Finding Hidden Cam in Hotel Bathroom," by Randy Kenner of the *Knoxville News-Sentinel*, a $1.5 million lawsuit was filed against a Knoxville hotel after a guest uncovered a video camera in a light. The guest originally believed the black dot he saw on the light fixture was an insect. When he attempted to kill the insect, he damaged the fixture and discovered the recording device. The camera, which turned on and off when the bathroom light switch was manipulated, did not appear to have been installed recently.

Don Wittkowski, a member of *The Press of Atlantic City*, wrote on another such instance in his article, "CCC Penalizes Two Men for Voyeurism in A.C." A casino in Atlantic City, New Jersey, received a $185,000 fine when it was discovered that a pair of surveillance officers, who are no longer employed by the casino, were using security cameras to inappropriately observe women, rather than to "ensure the integrity of the gaming operations," according to a spokesperson for the casino.

Another casino experienced a similar incident, which John Stearns details in his article for *The Arizona Republic,* "2 at Casino Fired for Breast Photos: Dealers, Customers Pictured." A number of females in the casino, the majority of whom were employees, had their chests photographed by a surveillance employee, with the support of his supervisor. These employees have since been terminated.

Nicole Howle of the *New York Injury News* writes of yet another incident, this time at a Walmart in Pennsylvania. The article, "Pennsylvania Employment Law Alert: Easton, PA Walmart Sued for Videotaping Inside a Bathroom," reveals how a lawsuit seeking over $500,000 was raised against the retail store after recording devices were found in a changing room and a unisex bathroom. The lawsuit alleges that the camera was installed in these rooms by a loss-prevention unit, which the store denies, as well as any charges that employee and customer rights to privacy were violated.

To avoid becoming "another story," the following security surveillance center checklist should be used to help aid in the decisions that need to be made when addressing the sensitive issues that are encountered in many workplaces. Remember, employees may challenge video surveillance for a wide variety of reasons—some of them based on federal laws, state laws, or court decisions. Since the laws and court decisions in this area can vary from state to state, the most important measure that one can take to avoid challenges to video surveillance is to consult with a knowledgable attorney before undertaking or conducting surveillance.

The following checklist is a good starting point and includes suggestions that may help avoid, or win, legal challenges to situations where video surveillance was obtained.

- Use video surveillance only when justified by a legitimate business purpose (i.e., investigating illegal conduct, investigating improper conduct, preventing theft, preventing workplace violence, etc.).
- Limit video surveillance to the least intrusive time, place, and method that will serve the business purpose.
- Use only visible cameras, or if covert cameras may be used, inform employees in writing that hidden cameras may be used.
- Obtain written employee consent to video surveillance for legitimate business purposes.
- Do not use video surveillance in areas where employees have a reasonable expectation of privacy (i.e., restrooms, locker rooms, dressing rooms, etc.).
- Do not use video surveillance devices that capture or record sound without complying with federal and state wiretap laws.
- In unionized workplaces, comply with any provisions in the collective bargaining agreement concerning video surveillance; if there are no such provisions, negotiate with the union before implementing video surveillance.
- Do not use video surveillance in connection with union activities.
- Do not use video surveillance in connection with any form of "concerted activity" by employees concerning terms or conditions of employment.
- Do not select employees for video surveillance in a manner that might be considered discriminatory under federal or state discrimination laws.
- Do not select employees for video surveillance in retaliation for exercising rights under any law.
- Determine what the state and local laws are regarding security surveillance center and video surveillance and comply with the laws.
- Train security surveillance center leaders and personnel in the legal issues involved in video surveillance.
- All information obtained through video surveillance should be treated as confidential.
- Limit access to video recordings to security surveillance center personnel and leaders on a "need-to-know" basis.
- Implement procedural safeguards to avoid unintended or improper use of security surveillance center recordings.

- Hidden or covert cameras are used by security surveillance centers to observe areas where surveillance cameras are not normally used or even expected to be placed. Covert cameras are installed to detect illicit activities. Many times these cameras are installed when information is received by the security surveillance center and are used to protect the assets of the company.
- The use of covert cameras may be limited or even prohibited in some countries, states, or by local governments. The use of covert cameras may be limited by industry, union contracts, or companies.
- Prior to installing a covert camera, make sure that it is legal to do so. Legal counsel should be obtained prior to using a covert camera.
- The severity of the suspected or alleged criminal activity should trigger the decision as to whether to use covert cameras. For example, suspected marijuana use by one or two individuals may not trigger the placement of a covert camera in some areas, but the sale of narcotics to employees may.
- If unsure if a covert camera should be used, it is usually better to err on the side of caution, and to seek legal counsel, only after you are sure it is 100% legal should a covert camera be used. If in doubt, leave it out.

When dealing with ethical dilemmas and how you address and respond to the wide variety of situations that come your way, remember the words of Mark Twain, "Always do right—this will gratify some and astonish the rest."

7 Audits, Thefts, and Effective Patrol Methods

It is important for security surveillance centers to stay abreast of new developments in the field and best practices to ensure that closed-circuit television (CCTV) monitoring and recording of activities are consistent with current standards and laws.

The principal objectives of the security surveillance center/CCTV monitoring and/or recording in public areas include the following:

- Enhancing guest, visitor, and employee safety
- Preventing and deterring employee and visitor misconduct
- Identifying misconduct by employees and visitors
- Identifying and gathering evidence
- Documenting employee actions to safeguard the rights of visitors and employees
- Reducing the cost and impact of guest and employee misconduct to the company
- Improving the allocation and deployment of security and safety measures in an effort to enhance the company's revenue and other assets
- CCTV monitoring and recording should be conducted in a professional, ethical, and legal manner.
- CCTV cameras may not be installed in any areas where there is reasonable expectation of privacy. These areas include locker rooms, dressing rooms, and bathrooms.
- Security surveillance center personnel using the CCTV camera system should be appropriately trained and supervised in the responsible use of the equipment located in the security surveillance center.
- Information obtained through monitoring and recording will only be released in accordance with company policy or as required by law.
- CCTV monitoring and recording of public areas should be conducted in a manner consistent with the law and company policies.
- CCTV monitoring of visitor and employee areas is limited to uses that do not violate the reasonable expectation of privacy as defined by the law.
- Violations of policy and procedures may result in disciplinary action and may subject those involved to criminal and civil liability under applicable state and federal laws.
- Packages leaving the property should be inspected and should be accompanied by a package pass. Only the items listed on the package pass are permitted to leave the property, and the pass must be signed by the appropriate property leader.

- Any deviation from these principles for inappropriate reasons (i.e., CCTV monitoring of guests or employees in a sexually suggestive manner, or monitoring solely based on race or gender) would undermine the acceptability of the security surveillance center resources for critical management goals and is strictly prohibited.

THE IMPORTANCE OF CCTV CAMERA AUDITS

The security surveillance center CCTV cameras should be audited on a regular basis and the results tracked. Each camera view should be inspected and verified via the live monitoring system to ensure that the picture quality is of a degree to identify subjects and is in the proper preset position. During the daily audit, an inspection of each camera should be conducted to ensure that each camera is recording properly and the recorded playback of each camera should also be conducted to ensure that it is playing back properly.

These audits should be conducted by a member of the security surveillance center team on a regular basis in a spreadsheet that lists the location, camera name, type of camera, date, time, person conducting audit, and issues. Also on the spreadsheet alongside the previous information, a section for resolution to any issue discovered should be listed. This resolution section should include date, time, person performing resolution, status, and outcome. The resolution cycle on any issue should continue until the situation is resolved.

Any camera that is not working properly should be repaired as soon as possible, especially in circumstances where a CCTV camera is the conduit for the protection of life and safety. In these situations, there is an expectation that the camera is working—and if the camera is in need of repair, the camera should be fixed immediately or taken out of service. It is true that the addition or use of CCTV cameras can be a great asset and force multiplier for any area; however, if the equipment is not maintained or the operators are poorly trained, it can become a burden and a liability.

An example of this circumstance is a camera in a guest elevator. Anyone getting into an elevator where there is a CCTV camera housing assumes that it is recording all activity in that elevator. In a worst-case scenario, if a person sees a CCTV camera in an elevator and becomes a victim of a crime, such as an assault, the person may allow the assault to occur believing that the CCTV camera is working and that the event is being viewed or at a minimum recorded, which will lead to the eventual identification and apprehension of the perpetrator. Failure to take a nonworking or poorly performing CCTV camera out of service could have catastrophic results impacting the victim, the property, and the establishment's reputation. The organization could be involved in legal action brought about from the victim's experience which could have a ripple effect on the corporation, business sector, or the entire industry.

During my career in law enforcement as a New Jersey State Trooper and a Municipal Police Officer in Clementon, New Jersey, unmanned police vehicles were beginning to be used on highways across the country to act as a deterrent. At the time, I had voiced an opinion that this could create a situation that could end badly if a person in need of police help had a choice to go to the unmanned marked vehicle or to another area. The logic is that if someone sees a marked police vehicle, the assumption is that there is a law enforcement official in the vehicle who can provide help. Imagine the catastrophic outcome if a person is running from people who are trying to cause harm and runs to a staged unoccupied police vehicle for help, which they believe to have an officer in it, and then become assaulted and harmed as a result.

The use of CCTV cameras that do not work or perform poorly can have the same effect and results to persons who are in need of assistance and have choices in deciding where to seek help. This is one reason why CCTV cameras should be repaired as quickly as possible, and dummy cameras (CCTV cameras that are not connected to anything) should not be used. As the years have gone by, I have noticed that both these strategies have decreased but unfortunately continue to be practiced.

Take, for example, an incident that occurred on the Bay Area Rapid Transit (BART) system on January 9, 2016, where a passenger on the train was shot and killed. According to an article released on January 20, 2016, by Chesley Brown, the security management company, titled, "BART Slaying Exposes Decoy Security Cameras."

There were no onboard videos of the crime, even though the transit agency had what appear to be surveillance cameras just feet from where the suspect shot the victim at close range. BART officials conceded that although all BART cars have what appears to be security cameras mounted to their ceilings, the vast majority of the devices are decoys incapable of capturing footage. It was reported that even some of their real cameras also failed to capture video as they were not working at the time of the shooting. The use of such dummy cameras is not common knowledge. Even one member of BART's board of directors said he was unaware of the decoys, and conceded that they amounted to a security gap in the Bay Area's backbone train system.

"This is deeply concerning," said Director Nick Josefowitz of San Francisco, who has been on the board about a year and did not know that some train cameras were decoys. "This is something we need to get to the bottom of."

A spokeswoman for the agency said working cameras will be on every car in BART's new fleet, the bulk of which will arrive between 2017 and 2021. At present, what appears to many riders to be sets of four cameras on the ceilings of each BART car are primarily fake cameras, an effort by agency officials to deter criminals, particularly vandals, without spending money on a more extensive surveillance system for soon-to-be replaced cars. BART Director Tom Radulovich of San Francisco, who has been on the board since 1996, said that when the cameras were installed on trains, directors knew some were not real. He said he couldn't recall the agency's rationale, but he assumed it was budgetary. "The thought was that they had a deterrent effect because some people thought they were real," he said. Since the September 11, 2001, terrorist attacks, more federal money has been available for transit security, he said, and BART has used some to buy new cameras. Radulovich said BART, knowing it was replacing its rail cars, may have chosen to install the new cameras in stations instead of aboard trains.

"I think some of the thinking," he said, "may have been, 'We're going to be getting new cars. Is this a good investment?'"

Although BART has many working cameras on platforms and in station lobbies, the fact that cameras inside trains are decoys comes with a cost, as some crimes and key incidents are not recorded. For instance, after a BART police officer shot and killed Oscar Grant early on New Year's Day 2009, investigators could not go back and view video of Grant getting into a scuffle on a train and then being pulled off the car by a second officer because there were no real security cameras on the train to record the incident."

In another article released by the *SF Gate* on January 14, 2016, written by Evan Sernoffsky, Michael Cabanatuan, and Demian Bulwa, titled, "BART Killing Exposes Security Gap—Many Train Cameras Are Decoys," the authors state:

BART police investigating the weekend killing of a passenger on a train in Oakland have no onboard video of the crime, even though the transit agency had what appear to be surveillance cameras just feet from where the suspect shot the victim at close range, *The Chronicle* has learned.

Although all BART cars have what look like cameras mounted to their ceilings, the vast majority of the devices are decoys incapable of capturing footage, BART officials conceded Wednesday. And some of the actual cameras are broken, two police sources said.

BART police said Wednesday that the suspect in the still-unsolved slaying was recorded before entering the train and after fleeing from it at the West Oakland station Saturday evening. They released clear photos taken by station cameras of a slim, tall man in a green jacket.

However, they released no images from inside the train. BART officials would not say why, but the two police sources, speaking on condition of anonymity, said no such footage exists—possibly because the cameras on the train were decoys.

Director in the dark

The use of such dummy cameras is not common knowledge. Even one member of BART's Board of Directors said he was unaware of the decoys, and conceded that they amounted to a security gap in the Bay Area's backbone train system. A spokeswoman for the agency said working cameras will be on every car in BART's new fleet, the bulk of which will arrive between 2017 and 2021. At present, what appear to many riders to be sets of four cameras on the ceilings of each BART car are primarily fakes, an effort by agency officials to deter criminals—particularly vandals – without spending money on a more extensive surveillance system for soon-to-be junked cars.

Although BART has many working cameras on platforms and in station lobbies, the fact that cameras inside trains are decoys comes with a cost, as some crimes and key incidents aren't preserved on film. For instance, after a BART police officer shot and killed Oscar Grant early on New Year's Day 2009, investigators could not go back and view video of Grant getting in a scuffle on a train and then being pulled off the car by a second officer. The reason is that no camera on the train recorded the incident.

'Very robust'

BART police declined to discuss the cameras Wednesday. At a news conference about the Saturday night killing, Police Chief Kenton Rainey said, "If you want to give me more resources, I'll take them."

Later, in an interview, Rainey said, "I'm not going to talk about our security system other than it is a very robust system. I don't know any other jurisdiction that has a robust system like this."

Even so, BART directors are expected to grill Rainey and General Manager Grace Crunican about surveillance at Thursday's board meeting in Oakland.

"This is deeply concerning," said Director Nick Josefowitz of San Francisco, who has been on the board about a year and didn't know that some train cameras were decoys. "This is something we need to get to the bottom of."

Suspect's movements

Rainey called Wednesday's news conference to release the surveillance photos of the suspect in Saturday's shooting, in which a man who boarded a San Francisco-bound train at Pittsburg/Bay Point Station shot another male passenger at about 7:40 p.m. as the train pulled into West Oakland.

The photos show the suspect entering Pittsburg/Bay Point Station and exiting West Oakland Station.

The alleged assailant—a slim, tall black man with a shaved head, wearing a green jacket with a hood, a backpack and beige work-style boots—ran from the train after the shooting. He was last seen across the street from West Oakland Station, by the 99 Cents Only store on Seventh Street.

BART police circulated a bulletin with photos of the suspect to other law enforcement agencies in the days after the killing, but did not release the images publicly until Wednesday. Rainey explained that police did not want to influence witnesses' descriptions of the killer.

No ID for victim

Authorities have struggled to identify the victim. Police said he appeared to be between 19 and 25 years old and was carrying no legitimate identification. The man, who died at the scene, had a knife when he was shot, officials said.

It's not yet known why the gunman opened fire, or even whether he knew the victim. Some BART riders expressed shock Wednesday when told of the decoy cameras. As he rode an afternoon train to Oakland for a public meeting on bay wetlands, San Francisco Supervisor Scott Wiener said, "I had no idea."

He added, "Video on transit is a pretty basic safety issue. When you have a problem, you want to go and find out what happened."

In 2009, Muni officials in San Francisco came under fire after an 11-year-old boy was stabbed on a city bus. Not all the coach's cameras were working, and an audit found that surveillance equipment on more than half of Muni buses and trains wasn't fully operational.

The agency scrambled to fix the problems. "We worked very hard to get better security on Muni," Wiener said. "It undermined our safety."

'Common trick'

Chronicle reporters walked the length of seven BART trains on Wednesday, taking note of the surveillance equipment. In all, 173 of 228 cameras on the cars—or 76 percent—appeared to be dummies.

Gerry Huth, a BART patron waiting for a train at Montgomery Street station, said, "I guess they're placebos. I've worked in warehousing and distribution for 25 years. It's a common trick."

But even in his line of work, Huth said, there are usually enough cameras to film an area.

"'If they're not covering an area properly, that's unacceptable," he said. "That's where it's a problem."

BART Director Tom Radulovich of San Francisco, who has been on the board since 1996, said that when the cameras were installed on trains, directors knew some were not real. He said he couldn't recall the agency's rationale, but he assumed it was budgetary. "The thought was that they had a deterrent effect because some people thought they were real," he said.

Since the Sept. 11 terrorist attacks, more federal money has been available for transit security, he said, and BART has used some to buy new cameras. Radulovich said BART, knowing it was replacing its rail cars, may have chosen to install the new cameras in stations instead of aboard trains.

"I think some of the thinking," he said, "may have been, 'We're going to be getting new cars. Is this a good investment?'"

In another related article released by the *San Francisco Chronicle* on January 24, 2016, written by Matier and Ross titled, "BARTs Damage-Control Scramble on Decoy Cameras," the authors state that,

BART didn't waste time announcing it would replace scores of dummy cameras on its trains with real ones—and with good reason.

The Chronicle report that embarrassed BART by revealing the decoy cameras hit just as the transit agency was putting pollsters into the field to gauge public support for a planned $3 billion bond measure to improve service and trains.

"It's damage control," said state Sen. Steve Glazer, D-Orinda, an outspoken critic of BART spending. "They have to convince the public that everything is going well when they go to the ballot."

Past polling has shown a majority of voters in San Francisco, Alameda and Contra Costa counties would be willing to back higher sales or property taxes to pay for BART improvements. But the support hovers just over the two-thirds threshold needed for passage.

Surveys have also shown that train safety and reliability are among BART riders' top concerns.

"They are really freaking out," one BART insider told us, referring to management's fear that the camera fiasco could help sink public confidence in the agency.

BART spokeswoman Alicia Trost doesn't dispute that *The Chronicle*'s report brought a trainload of public heat.

"The last thing we want is for riders to not feel they are safe, and we made the decision to get rid of the decoys altogether and make a very public announcement that we are buying the cameras," Trost said.

Just how fast BART will get them and how it will pay for them isn't known, she said.

Apart from video cameras, BART has been working to put live-streaming cameras on its trains since the agency won a $3.8 million federal homeland security grant in 2010. Much of the equipment is still boxed up in storage, though—last year, BART fired the company it had hired for this and other work.

Trost said BART still hopes to have live-streaming cameras "on a very select number of trains, in a limited area"—"possibly by September."

The bottom line is that on Saturday, January 9, 2016, at approximately 7:45 PM, a murder took place that stemmed from a shooting on an SFO Airport bound train, approaching the West Oakland Station that killed one person.

- Approximately 76% of cameras installed throughout the BART station and on its trains are actually decoys that are incapable of recording incidents, and some of the actual cameras are broken, which adds to the challenge of solving crimes.
- The BART agency won a $3.8 million federal homeland security grant in 2010. Much of the equipment is still boxed up in storage, though—last year, BART fired the company it had hired for this and other work.

- Approximately 6 years have elapsed since the $3.8 million federal home-land security grant.

From the articles that you have read, would you say that BART is negligent or has been derelict in their duties to protect the public, or do you feel that they have met the industry standard?

Either way you decide—my hope is that this example clearly illustrates:

- Why I believe the use of dummy cameras is risky
- The negative impact an incident can have on any company or organization that makes a conscious decision to use dummy cameras
- The importance of the repair and upkeep of CCTV cameras and equipment is paramount, especially when placed in areas pertaining to safety and security
- There is an expectation from the public that an overt camera be a real camera and in good working order

Amazingly, I have had conversations with executive leaders who have wanted to use dummy cameras throughout my career, sometimes weeks after tragic incidents have occurred in the community where dummy cameras were used. Many times leadership has wanted to place a dummy camera with a sign indicating that the area was monitored by CCTV. The belief from executive leadership was that this would be a great deterrent. My position has always been to strongly advise against implementing this measure and explained why, by using the previously listed information to support my argument. In the end of these types of discussion, the decision has always been to place an active camera with the CCTV signage, instead of using a dummy camera. Remember that you are the expert in this area and that leadership will come to you for direction, guidance, and answers pertaining to the protection of assets and the important role of the security surveillance center.

When a CCTV camera is not working and is located in a high-risk area, it should be fixed as soon as possible. If it is unable to be fixed, then it should be removed. Critical areas should be established by the property leaders and communicated to the security surveillance center leadership team. If a CCTV camera is not functioning properly in a guest area where there is an expectation that it is functioning properly and it is not able to be removed, the occupants of the area should be made aware that it is not functioning. This can be done in a number of ways; it can be removed, it can be covered by a drawstring bag or a box crafted by the maintenance department along with signage indicating that it is out of service. The area should be inspected and patrolled regularly to ensure that the previous measures are in place and to provide a safe environment. These patrols should be documented in the daily activity log.

In noncritical areas where CCTV cameras are not performing to the standard or are not working, they should be repaired as soon as possible. An example of a noncritical area would be a camera at a point of sale (POS) that is discovered to be underperforming during a time when the outlet is closed. Let's say the outlet is not scheduled to open again for 2 days. This repair should be prioritized, and it should be completed before the outlet is scheduled to open again.

In circumstances where there are other, more pertinent critical CCTV cameras in the queue for repair, they should be repaired first—and the POS CCTV camera should be moved down on the priority list, but repaired prior to the opening of the outlet.

The CCTV cameras and system should be maintained and inspected on a regular schedule. For example, CCTV camera domes should be scheduled to be cleaned on a regular basis. If CCTV cameras are used in a seasonal capacity in certain areas, those areas should have one cycle of their maintenance scheduled a relatively short time before the season begins in order to certify that all CCTV cameras and equipment are working properly.

The security surveillance center should always have a regular power source and a redundant power source, usually a generator that is used to create emergency power during a power outage. Although, if a property is fortunate enough to be located where there is the ability to obtain power from two regular power sources, they should take advantage of this option. For example, in the event that the regular power source (A) is not working, a plan and process should occur that allows for an instant transition to regular power source (B). In the event that both regular power sources (A) and (B) become unavailable, power source (C) should transition to the emergency backup power.

Over the years, I have been personally involved in many power outages at various properties across the country as a result of hurricanes, severe weather, electric grids going out of service, and property issues. Some of the best practices implemented over the years include the following: The inspection of the emergency power supply systems including the generators and fuel tanks that supply the energy source for emergency backup power. Frequent inspections and testings are necessary to ensure that they are full and that the generators are in proper working order. These inspections should occur on a regular basis throughout the year, and the frequency should increase when there are alerts for severe weather. This way when an event occurs and the system is activated, it will perform as expected. Also, an agreement should be reached with a local fuel supplier for the delivery of emergency fuel to ensure that deliveries will occur during a major event or that a fuel tanker will be delivered on site for the needs of the property.

The following are protocols and procedures that should be implemented or become part of the established routine of security surveillance center personnel.

- Maintain good physical access controls to the security surveillance center. Everyone entering should have a reason or a purpose to do so. All visitors should sign in and sign out. The information gathered should include name, date, arrival time, departure time, purpose of visit, signature, and badge number.
- Anyone entering the security surveillance center should have a purpose and reason for being in this sensitive area. Only those authorized should be permitted.
- Visitors should follow sign-in procedures.
- All computers should be secured.

When security surveillance personnel are conducting proactive patrols and researching the POS areas in an effort to develop cases for employee investigative interviews, they should look for the following indicators of employee theft or fraud:

- Unsecured computers and points of sale
- Employee does not generate a receipt
- Employee does not give a receipt to a customer
- Employee is constantly counting money or counting his or her bank down
- Employee uses managers or supervisors to swipe card
- When coupons are received, the employee does not record them immediately but puts them to the side for later use
- Review no-sale or void lists, then compare to CCTV coverage for that employee, location, date, and time to determine the type of transaction that occurred

Another area in which security surveillance center personnel can conduct proactive patrols to develop cases for employee investigative interviews are the back-of-house areas. For example, the receiving area of any property is critical for the operation of all departments. The receiving area inspects deliveries and either accepts or rejects them. The employee receiving the items should verify that the order is the correct amount, the quality of the product meets standards, and the item is delivered at the right time and location. Employees who receive product should be aware of excess ice, watered-down products, wrapping paper, and packaging that can add dead weight, which is sometimes referred to as the "tare weight," from the gross weight in order to compute the net weight of the merchandise. The employee receiving the product should also inspect the product for damage, including checking the quality under the top layer, to ensure that all succeeding layers are equal to the facing layer. Employees who receive product should also be wary of delivery persons eager to help them carry the delivered items to their storage areas.

Receivers should watch for incomplete shipments, as well as for the delivery person who asks them to sign for a complete order after telling them that the rest of the order will arrive later. If this should occur, the two options are to not accept the order or to make a detailed note on the form being signed of what was received and what is pending delivery.

The following are indicators of employee theft or fraud in the warehouse or areas that receive goods and products:

- Employee does not inspect or weigh items upon arrival to the loading dock or warehouse. Receivers of products should beware of excess ice, wrapping paper, and packaging that can add weight, which is referred to as the tare weight. This amount should be subtracted from the gross weight to determine the net weight.
- Employee does not inventory items when received or when issued to departments. For example, food and culinary departments should perform a check and balance with the warehouse and receiving areas to confirm that what was ordered was actually delivered.

- Delivery of orders to departments by employee are damaged, poor quality, or missing items.

In addition to the security surveillance center auditing the warehouse and receiving areas, the following are measures that should be implemented to deter theft and fraud from these areas:

- Employee vehicles are not to be parked near the warehouse or receiving areas. If observed, CCTV coverage should be reviewed.
- If a vendor is authorized to have direct access to an area, the vendor should be escorted by an employee.
- When product is delivered, the steps taken by those accepting the delivery should include the following:
  - Check that the product matches the requisition.
  - Check that the quantity matches the requisition.
  - Inspect the product to ensure that it is in good condition.
  - Weigh the goods and/or products.
  - After these steps are completed, accept and verify the product immediately.
  - If a vendor is authorized to have direct access to an area, the vendor should be escorted by an employee, and all goods and/or products should be verified prior to the storage of any goods and/or products.

The staging of items is another tactic used by the dishonest or disgruntled employees to commit theft from a company. How this works is that the employee places items in an area that is located by the exits or close to the outer perimeter of a facility. Employees will stage items near or place them in these areas to retrieve at a later time. Sometimes they will even throw the item over a fence to be picked up by someone else while they are working.

Another often overlooked area where employees stage items are the trash and recycling dumpsters. Parking should be prohibited in this area. One method of theft in this area occurs when an employee simply places an item in the dumpster and comes back at a later time to retrieve the item. If the dumpster is located in an area that has public access—the employee can simply call a friend to retrieve the item while he or she is working. This is why it is important to place cameras in these areas to provide coverage and to help establish CCTV evidence for a case.

I have often commented that if you want to learn about what is going on at a property, ask the person or department that is responsible for emptying the trash cans of the executive leadership of any property. It is amazing the amount of sensitive information that is not shredded and is simply thrown into a trash can. This is why I recommend a policy that all sensitive information be shredded by a cross-cut shredder before it is disposed. Unsecured computers are another method through which unscrupulous people can obtain information. To protect information on computers, it is a good practice to lock screens and screen savers anytime the user gets up and walks away.

JUST DOESN'T LOOK RIGHT

One of the most valuable tools of security surveillance center personnel is the power of observation and the ability to piece that together with actions taken by those under observation to recognize when something "just doesn't look right" (JDLR). For example, a personal story of JDLR in action occurred during my rookie year as a local law enforcement officer in Clementon, New Jersey. Late at night, my lieutenant and I were on patrol when I observed a white male carrying a milk crate with some items in it. My instincts told me that this just doesn't look right, and I advised the lieutenant of the observation. The patrol vehicle was turned around, and the subject who was walking down the sidewalk immediately placed the crate on the ground when he saw the patrol vehicle. The subject advised that he found the items contained in the crate—stereo equipment—in a dumpster and was taking the stereo equipment home. At that time, a report came in from dispatch that a nearby home was burglarized and—you guessed it—stereo equipment was missing. The subject admitted to stealing the stereo equipment, and the rest as they say is history.

This is one example of how JDLR and the observer's instincts can be used as a method of detection by security surveillance center personnel. JDLR takes into account all of the information that a security surveillance center operator has at the time of the observation. Experiences observing people, time spent actively observing others at work or leisure, and life experiences are drawn from to make a JDLR conclusion. The JDLR concept puts everything together so that security surveillance center personnel can make an observation and immediately identify when something, someone, or some action just doesn't look right. As security surveillance center personnel become more experienced and encounter more situations, they learn to recognize normal behavior and actions regarding certain events or interactions. When behaviors and actions deviate from the standard or normal response to a situation, then further investigation and observation are necessary. Sometimes the activities will be nothing at all and can be explained away. However, other times the keen observation by security surveillance center personnel leads to bigger things that enable actions to be taken to prevent or catch someone involved with violating policy, procedure, or committing criminal activity.

As previously discussed, JDLR is a powerful tool in the recognition of behaviors and activities that provide security surveillance center personnel a signal of those about to violate policy, procedure, or commit criminal activity. The following are examples of behavior or actions that a cashier at a POS would exhibit that fall into the category of JDLR:

- The cashier fails to enter a transaction or enters the transaction after the customer leaves.
- The cashier sets aside payment or puts money from the payment into his or her pocket.
- The cashier does not issue a receipt or throws it away.
- The cashier sets aside or stores a receipt for later use.
- The cashier overcharges customers, keeps a record, and steals money at a later time. People who conduct this type of theft will often keep a record

through the use of coins, paperclips, straws, and so on, by placing them in an area that they can see easily. These items represent a specific amount of money, and doing this helps them to keep track of how much money they can "safely" steal without having a large variance in their cash drawer.

- The cashier works out of an open drawer.
- The cashier undercharges or does not charge friends or relatives. For example, when reviewing the cashier transactions on CCTV, the following may be observed:
  - A large purchase is made, and a small amount of money is exchanged between guest and cashier. Also, in the event a credit card was used, programs are available that track the transactions at a POS. These should be reviewed to see exactly how much was charged for a particular purchase.
- No money or credit card will be seen being exchanged between guest and cashier.
- The cashier voids legitimate transactions, sometimes referred to as line voids.
- The cashier sells the customer an item for the correct amount, rings it as a lower-priced item, and pockets the difference.
- The cashier commingles company funds with personal monies. Besides a policy regarding this type of behavior, another way to help prevent this is to establish a maximum amount of cash an employee may have on his or her person. For example, if the policy is that the most money an employee can have on his or her person is $20 and the employee has more, which if a person is committing this act they will, it is a violation of policy and should lead to an investigative interview of the subject.
- The cashier frequently counts down his or her register or cash drawer. Again, a policy clearly stating that register and cash drawers will only be counted down at specific times will benefit the company. For example, the counting down of a register or cash drawer should only be permitted when starting at a register or cash drawer and when finished working at a register or cash drawer under the destination of the security surveillance center.
- There is unauthorized use of a manager's card.
- The cashier requests or uses printouts of receipts listing total sales.
- The cashier counts bank away from others and cameras.
- There is unusual refund activity. The use of programs that are available to track the transactions at a POS will display this type of activity. Once identified, security surveillance center personnel should review CCTV coverage to determine if refund activity was legitimate.
- The cashier conceals money on person. For example, puts money in his or her pocket and leaves the area.

The following pertains to food and beverage areas, the types of thefts that occur, and proactive methods to combat theft in these areas. It is estimated that 5 cents of every dollar of revenue generated in the food and beverage industry at bars and restaurants is stolen, 4 of the 5 cents that is stolen is stolen by employees. Food and beverage areas are largely cash businesses, and this contributes to the thefts.

Other areas of vulnerability in this area include poor controls, improper segregation of duties, and inventory that is easily hidden, removable, and consumable. For example, food and beverages, including alcoholic beverages, are highly transportable and once stolen, the owner of the items is almost impossible to identify.

Theft in the food and beverage area can occur in a variety of ways. The methods used are only limited by one's imagination. Cash theft, or embezzlement, usually involves a transaction between a guest and an employee, although it can occur without guest interaction. One way, as I have seen in the past, that this occurs is when bold employees simply steal the money from another employee's cash register. The opportunity generally presents itself to the thief when employees do not follow policy, procedure, or internal controls. In these cases, the employee who has the money stolen leaves his or her cash drawer open after a transaction and the rogue employee simply takes the money out of the register when the cashier is not looking. Other methods used to steal funds by employees who operate a cash register include the following:

- Cashier collects cash for product from guest, provides receipt and cancels or voids the transaction.
- Cashier collects cash for product from a guest and records the sale as a guest walkout.
- Cashier collects cash for product from guest, steals the cash, and uses a coupon to complete the transaction.
- Cashier removes funds from the cash drawer.
- Cashier gives away product.
- Cashier does not record the sale or transaction.

We will review the methods that can be used to help identify these types of theft, but first let's explore some of the ways that thieves keep track of unrecorded sales. Basically, they can use a variety of items to keep track of their theft from a POS. These items can include change, toothpicks, etc., where each item represents a different denomination of currency. Thieves also keep track of unrecorded sales by placing a specific coin into an empty slot in the cash drawer for each dollar taken. When more than one person has access to the same register, the thieves will sometimes place the cash to be stolen from the register face down and cash to remain in the register face up. Then when the opportunity presents itself, they steal the money that is face down from the cash register. Another method is to simply use a calculator that is kept near the cash register to track unrecorded sales.

There are a variety of ways that thieves try to disguise the removal of funds from a cash register. It is important to try to eliminate or reduce the opportunities that an employee, with bad intent, has to steal from the cash register. One way is to make sure that the cashier is not permitted to comingle the funds from the cash register with their personal money. If this is permitted, it gives the cashier the ability to disguise his or her actions by making it easier to steal the funds from the cash register and put the stolen cash in his or her pocket. Another method used is when the cashier counts the cash register drawer down out of CCTV camera view. While out of camera view, the employee steals the funds from the cash drawer. Another area of risk is when the funds are being returned from the cash register location to the cash control area where the employee receives and returns the money bag. To help prevent theft during this process, the policies and procedures should state that money must be counted under CCTV camera view and that cashiers will follow a predetermined route when carrying funds to and from the cash control area to the work location. During the transit of these funds, the entire route should be under CCTV camera view, and no stops are permitted along the way. Remember when it comes to this type of theft, it is important to follow the money.

Lack of proper controls also contributes to concerns in these areas. The more of the following control issues that exist in an area, the higher opportunity and likelihood that the percentage of theft will increase:

- Constantly operating under a state of stress
- Inadequate financial controls
- Management and employees who are unethical or dishonest
- Employees aware of lack of CCTV camera coverage
- Vendor/employee relationships

The following are some things to look for when conducting due diligence patrols following the identify, observe, and understand (IOU) method in the area of cashier theft and fraud. Many times voided transactions will be used in an attempt to conceal or disguise theft. For our purposes, a legitimate voided transaction is caused by a computer malfunction or human error. Thieves use the voided transaction function to conceal an actual sale and steal money. For example, I had a case where a cashier had the ability to perform line voids on the cash register without needing a supervisor or anyone else to approve the void. The cashier would ring up the sale and process the transaction, then line void the transaction, steal the money, and process the next transaction properly. The amount a cashier can steal in a short period of time can add up quickly, in this case it was tens of thousands of dollars over a period of time. This is why it is important that proper controls exist and that there is a separation of duties between those who perform the void transaction and those who approve them.

The normal life cycle of a transaction process in food and beverage areas between guests and cashiers in which orders are placed should occur as follows. The order is taken from the guest and is entered into the POS system. The order is received in the kitchen. The order is prepared and delivered to the guest. In this process, it is important that kitchen personnel do not prepare or serve any items without an order originating from the POS system. It is important that policy, procedures, and controls are instituted that address the issue of any items served without originating from the POS system; if this occurs, it must have proper authorization. The opportunity to commit fraud and theft can occur when the cashier resells an entire order to another customer by holding onto a receipt and stealing the money from that transaction. When a different customer orders the same thing, the cashier does not enter it into the POS system and has the cook complete the order without the receipt. The cashier then uses the same receipt that was generated for the first customer for the order placed by the second customer. This results in the product being served twice, but only entered and paid into the POS system once.

We discussed some of the ways that theft can occur in food, beverage, and POS areas. The following are some of the methods the security surveillance center should utilize to uncover suspicious activities and dishonest employees. Employee theft and fraud often occur at the POS locations. Why? Let me borrow a quote attributed to famous bank robber Willie Sutton, "Because that's where the money is." The installation of CCTV cameras over POS locations is paramount in detecting theft, reducing losses, and providing a deterrent effect.

The daily review of variance reports and exception reports is critical to the effective monitoring of cash handling employees. The use of the CCTV system, cameras placed over the POS locations, in conjunction with variance and exception reports acts as a force multiplier in terms of the security surveillance center investigating these cases. Comparing the CCTV coverage with the details of the variance and exception reports will determine if the transaction was conducted with bad intent or was legitimate.

All significant variances and voids should be investigated to determine if there are any repetitive patterns, that proper authorization levels were utilized, and if fraud or theft was committed by the employee. Frequent cash overages and shortages can be signs of fraud and theft. Cash overages could indicate that the employee was unable to keep track of the money needed to be removed from the cash drawer in order to reconcile the cash drawer, whereas cash shortages can be an indicator of an employee committing theft directly from the cash drawer. The cash shortage could also be a result of an employee losing track of the money needed to be removed from the cash drawer in order to reconcile the cash drawer.

IDENTIFY, OBSERVE, AND UNDERSTAND

An acronym that best describes the process that security surveillance center personnel should use to detect, respond, investigate, and gather the evidence needed for an incident or event is IOU. Identify, Observe, and Understand is one of the most effective methods to detect policy violations, suspicious activity, and crime. The IOU method is also useful in consistently identifying persons of interest who require further observation and investigation. An IOU patrol generally begins at a specific location, such as a POS terminal, and each person in the area is *identified* as a guest or employee. All observations should be recorded so that if anything needs to be referred or investigated at a later date, it will be available. The next step in the IOU method of patrol is to *observe* the activity looking for criminal activity, violations of policies, procedures, or internal controls. The final step in the IOU method of patrol is to *understand* the activity or action being observed. If anything appears suspicious, criminal activity, violations of policies, procedures, or internal controls are observed, then further observation and investigation must occur. Only after security surveillance center personnel *understand* what is going on and everything appears normal should the IOU patrol of the next area begin. Remember that the area under observation should stay under observation until security surveillance center personnel *understand* what the particulars of the activity being *observed* are and what the proper response to the activity should be.

TRI-SHOT

If during the IOU patrol an event or activity is observed that appears suspicious or unusual, tri-shot coverage should be instituted to obtain information that can be used to make informed decisions, conduct investigations, or use as evidence at a later date. Tri-shot coverage consists of a minimum of three specific views of an incident or event. One of the tri-shot views is an unobstructed overview of the incident. The second is a specific view used to monitor a specific area. The third is an identification view used to identify the people involved in the incident or event. These views answers the questions of who was present during, before, and after the incident or event and what the degree of involvement was of each person. It is important to set up the tri-shot as soon as an incident or event is deemed suspicious or unusual.

AUDITS

Another key tool that the security surveillance center should use to detect violations of policies, procedures, internal controls, and theft is audits. Audits are useful to monitor transactions and processes in key areas like the POS locations. Prior to conducting an audit, the personnel assigned should review all information, documentation, policies, procedures, CCTV, etc. Persons of interest, work schedules, parameters of the audit, and who is authorized to know about the audit should be discussed prior to the beginning of the audit. Auditors usually conduct research and investigate suspicious activity, criminal activity, and violations of policy and procedure.

Security surveillance center personnel are usually called upon to conduct a close watch observation on specific subjects. Close watches are generally generated when specific information is received regarding suspicious or criminal activity being conducted by specific individuals in specific areas. The close watch monitors every move the individual makes while on property. Close watches can be generated from a variety of sources, including the general manager, president, department leaders, employees, etc. Close watches can be very time consuming. For example, a close watch of an employee would entail coverage of a person as soon as he or she entered the property until he or she left the property for the day.

For a close watch to be successful, it should include the following:

- When the information is initially received, gather as many of the facts as possible. Who, what, when, where, why, and how should be answered.
- Treat all requests for a close watch seriously, regardless of who is reported to be involved.
- Gather case facts including photos, schedules, policy, and procedures, and create a case file.
- Assign the person best suited to perform the close watch after being supplied specific details. As I like to say, "Put the round peg into the round hole."

- Assign a member of the security surveillance center leadership team to oversee and be accountable for the close watch.
- Periodically check on the status of the close watch, at a minimum check status on a daily basis in order to keep abreast of any developments or details.

Covert or hidden cameras should only be used by the security surveillance center when authorized by the leader of the department. This type of camera is generally used to observe areas that cannot be observed by the regular CCTV system. Hidden or covert cameras are usually installed to detect illicit activities based on credible information received by the security surveillance center. Be very careful when using covert cameras. Make sure that their use is not limited or prohibited in any way, shape, or form. Be sure to check with the legal entity of your company before using a covert camera. Even then, make sure it is *not* used in restrooms, locker rooms, or any area where an individual may expect a reasonable right to privacy. If there is ever any doubt, leave it out.

8 Training

Before any training program can begin, the focus of selecting people to be part of the security surveillance center team must occur. The selection of candidates and the training of security surveillance center personnel are among the most important aspects of this area. Being a member of the security surveillance center should be a coveted position of which, in the proper environment, one should not merely apply for a job, but is invited to join the team. It is important to invest the time, money, and resources into the training of security surveillance center personnel for many reasons, including the safety of guests, visitors, employees, and the protection of company assets. A well-selected and well-trained security surveillance center will ultimately help to improve profit margins by identifying and detecting suspicious activity and those committing these acts.

Candidates who wish to become part of the security surveillance center team should have the ability to interact, have the ability to communicate well with others, and have the aptitude to develop the skill set needed for the position. When selecting candidates, remember that it is generally easier for a person who has the aptitude and ability to learn the skills of the security surveillance center than it is for a person to learn how to genuinely provide internal guest service and interact and communicate well with others. The security surveillance center professional must possess an innate ability to interact and genuinely communicate with others. "When in doubt—don't hire—keep looking," said Jim Collins.

This concept is reinforced in the book, *Good to Great*, by Jim Collins, which supports the notion that hiring the right talent has more to do with innate character traits and innate capabilities than with specific knowledge, background, or skills. The following are some other key concepts pertaining to the hiring process presented by author Jim Collins.

"Get the right people on the bus ... and then figure out where to drive it."

"The purpose of compensation is not to 'motivate' the right behaviors from the wrong people, but to keep the right people in the first place."

"The old adage 'People are your most important asset' is wrong. People are not your most important asset. The right people are."

Once the right people are "on the bus," it is important for the leaders of the security surveillance center team to communicate and practice the following:

- An open-door policy
- The inverted pyramid philosophy
- Frederick Herzberg's Hygiene Theory
- Douglas McGregor's Theory X and Theory Y

An open-door policy and the inverted pyramid philosophy go hand in hand with developing a sense of esprit de corps in which enthusiasm, devotion, and a strong regard for the performance of the security surveillance center team are established. I have always practiced these philosophies and ensured that the teams that I have worked with knew that those on the front line and in the trenches are the most important assets of the department and that they have the ability to make the team look great—or not. It was also clearly communicated that although leadership does include management by walking around in the daily duties; the day-to-day operations and the routine interactions with others are spearheaded by those on the front line.

Frederick Herzberg's Hygiene Theory states that the opposite of satisfaction is not dissatisfaction, but rather, no satisfaction. Hygiene factors can move someone from dissatisfaction to no satisfaction. The following are examples of hygiene factors:

- Physical work conditions
- Surroundings
- Salary
- Coworkers
- External factors
- Motivation factors

Only motivators can move someone to satisfaction. The following are examples of motivators:

- Achievement
- Recognition
- Responsibility
- Satisfaction from work itself
- (Money is not a motivator)

In creating a successful and productive environment, it is important that the leaders of the security surveillance center recognize these motivators during the selection process and in the day-to-day operation of the security surveillance center.

Douglas McGregor's Theory X and Theory Y are based on two types of people called X and Y. The following are examples of characteristics that make up these categories.

Theory X

- People are not ambitious.
- People prefer to be directed.
- People resist change.
- People have no interest in organizational goals.
- People will attempt to avoid work whenever possible.

Theory Y

- People are creative.
- Ingenuity is common.

- People have the capacity for creativity.
- Work can be as natural as play.
- People have genuine caring/emphatic skills.

Obviously, the characteristics exhibited in Theory Y are of those who would excel in the security surveillance center environment.

The present-day security surveillance center professional is expected to be knowledgeable of all areas, and the public perception of interactions with internal and external guests should be seamless. The concept of getting the "right people on the bus, and then in the right seats" is key to the overall success of any security surveillance center that wishes to be a strong service provider, leader, and innovator in the field. The leadership team of the security surveillance center must recognize what motivates the members of their team. The opposite of satisfaction is not dissatisfaction, but rather, no satisfaction. Remember to focus on the motivating factors that can move someone to satisfaction. Energies should also be focused on people who possess those characteristics exhibited in McGregor's Theory Y in order to be successful.

Finally, the day arrives when the team has been selected, the security surveillance center is completed, and all of the equipment is installed and functioning properly. Training of all of the security surveillance center personnel should commence and be continuous and ongoing. This is a key principle and factor in determining how successful the operation will be. This also helps prevent the occurrence where a person has 10 years in the business but only 1 year of experience, because after the first year he or she did not continue to train, learn, and educate himself or herself and keep abreast of the ever-changing best practices, technologies, and laws.

As a leader, it is important to lead by example and stress the importance of training and learning. Personnel cannot be expected to perform at their optimum level if not trained and exposed to pertinent relevant material. Once the initial on-board training of personnel is completed, periodic training sessions should be scheduled and made mandatory. The training should consist of material that is current, specific, and deals with personnel concerns and issues. For example, reoccurring errors or questions should be one focus of the training sessions. Otherwise, if these areas are not addressed, it could have a negative impact on the morale of the team and possibly result in a serious mistake that could have catastrophic results.

Training is a cyclical process that should continually be updated to meet the needs and concerns of the security surveillance center. Training is not an end, but rather, is an ongoing approach to continually acquire knowledge and skills. There are many areas that should be addressed in training. These areas range from the general to the specific. The qualities that security surveillance center personnel should possess to be successful in this area should include the ability to multitask, to remain calm in stressful situations, to make good decisions, and to be able to communicate clearly and concisely. The training needed for security surveillance center personnel depends on the setting and environment. At a minimum, security surveillance center personnel should receive the following:

- Training in the legal, technical, and ethical parameters of appropriate camera use
- Training in the operation of CCTV cameras, skills, and techniques

- A copy of the security surveillance center policy and procedures
- Written acknowledgment that the contents of the policy and procedures of the security surveillance center have been read and the contents are understood
- Policies and procedures of all areas

The following types of cameras and equipment that are available for the operation of a security surveillance center should include the following:

- Fixed cameras
- Pan–tilt–zoom (PTZ) cameras
- Black and white cameras
- Color cameras
- Digital cameras
- Digital recorders

The security surveillance center personnel should know what the limitations of the cameras are, what the cameras can do, and where they are permitted to be installed. The following should be included in the dissemination of this information:

- What are the differences between a fixed camera and a PTZ camera?
- What are the best applications for fixed cameras?
- What are the best applications for PTZ cameras?
- What is the difference between an overview shot and a close-up shot, and when should each be used?
- What is a tri-shot, and when should it be utilized?
- CCTV cameras cannot be installed in areas where there is an expectation of privacy (i.e., restrooms and changing rooms).
- It is best to keep a wide-angle shot of incidents, especially when personnel are responding to an incident. The wide angle allows the entire scene to be captured and identifies people who are involved or in the vicinity of the situation.

The security surveillance center personnel should understand the importance of the proper setup and monitor display of the CCTV systems. The explanation of why this is critical to the operation and patrols conducted by security surveillance center personnel should include the following:

- It creates a productive, effective, and efficient security surveillance center environment.
- An effective security surveillance center bases its setups and monitor displays on property needs and the frequency of types of incidents and crimes.
- Identification of high-risk and vulnerable areas is a determining factor of the day-to-day setup of the monitor display of the CCTV systems in the security surveillance center.
- For the protection of the internal and external guest, it is recommended that entrances, exits, heavily traveled corridors, and back of the house areas be set up on the monitor displays in the security surveillance center.

- Deterrence, identification of suspects, development of leads for investigations, and timely responses are some of the positive effects of the proper setup and monitor displays of the CCTV system in the security surveillance center.
- CCTV cameras should be set up so that they return to their predetermined positions, or their "at-rest" positions, when not in use. This enables security surveillance center personnel to locate and track subjects and identify incidents in an efficient, effective, and timely manner.

The following is an outline of some of the areas of responsibility that security surveillance center personnel should receive training on and be able to demonstrate a high proficiency level when completed. Security surveillance center personnel should be well versed in the detection techniques utilized for the identification of violations of policy, procedure, and the law. These detection techniques should include the following:

- Identify, observe, and understand (IOU) patrols
- Just doesn't look right (JDLR)
- Use of tri-shot techniques when gathering information, observing an incident, or conducting investigations
- Regular and routine audits of key areas of operations
- Investigations of violations of policy and procedures to determine if the person was attempting to steal or if the violation was accidentally committed

The duties of security surveillance center personnel include the following:

- Relieve outgoing security surveillance center personnel of all duties, responsibilities, assignments, and equipment. Ascertain what incidents or investigations occurred during the previous shift, which may have an impact, relevance, or effect on the personnel arriving on duty.
- Make sure all outgoing security surveillance center personnel are relieved from the previous shift, and that any assignments are turned over to the oncoming shift. If any assignments are unable to be reassigned due to staffing needs or other issues, a member of the security surveillance center leadership team must be contacted immediately.
- Advise oncoming security surveillance center personnel of any correction, addition, or change in posts, assignments, or details.
- Perform security surveillance center dispatcher duties.
- Maintain a daily summary of all security surveillance center–related activities. Activities and incidents that should be documented include the following:
  - Alarms activity and responses
  - Incidents involving guests
  - Incidents involving employees
  - Notifications made to emergency services, fire department, police, etc.

- Responses to the property by emergency services, fire department, police, etc.
- Conduct a CCTV camera check and document any discrepancies or areas that are not in proper working order. Notify a member of the security surveillance center leadership team with findings.
- Maintain accountability of radios assigned to security surveillance center personnel. When using a radio, remember to
  - Stay calm
  - Speak in a clear, calm voice
  - Do not shout
  - Provide name or call sign, location, and nature of call
- Maintain, inspect, and accurately complete the key control log. Entries should be written in a neat and legible manner. Any errors are to have a line drawn through the error, preferably in red ink, and initialed. The proper entry is to be recorded on the next line of the ledger. The key log should include the following:
  - Who issued the key
  - Who received the key
  - When the key was issued
  - When the key was returned
  - Who received the key
  - Who returned the key
- Monitor all alarm systems. In the event of any alarm activation, dispatch appropriate personnel to the location and contact the appropriate outside agencies if needed.
- Communications with others should include the following:
  - *Be sincere*: Make eye contact and let the person know he or she has your undivided attention.
  - *Smile*: Conveys a sense of respect and that the discussion is important to you.
  - *Listen*: Actively listen to what is being communicated. Some ways to demonstrate that one is listening actively include nodding and responding verbally at appropriate times in the conversation. Also, ask questions or gather more facts when there is a natural break in the conversation.
  - *Speak*: Address others in a clear, calm, and respectful tone.
  - *Stay focused*: On the conversation and the situation at hand. Do not get side tracked or on tangents that do not pertain to the discussion.
- Coordinate all radio traffic related to the security surveillance center.
- Coordinate all telephone communications that are received at the security surveillance center.
- Perform duties in a professional, courteous, efficient, and effective manner.

Paperwork is to be organized, accurate, and completed by the end of each shift. In the event that paperwork will not be completed by the end of a shift, a member of the security surveillance center leadership team must be notified.

A list regarding an overview of the security surveillance center training, duties and responsibilities should include the following:

- Introduction to the security surveillance center
  - Review purpose and mission of the security surveillance center
  - Review policies and procedures
  - Review organizational structure
  - Introductions - Each member provides a brief background to the team regarding experience, etc.
  - Review of the job description and expectations.
  - Review Just Doesn't Look Right (JDLR)
  - Review Identify, Observe and Understand (IOU)
  - Review Tri-Shot coverage
  - Review the open-door policy
  - Review inverted pyramid concept and management style
  - Review work schedules and processes regarding availability
- Overview of the security surveillance center
  - Review daily operations and processes
  - Review job functions and roles
  - Review the proper use of security surveillance center tools and equipment
  - Review proper monitoring and operation of security surveillance center cameras and the CCTV system
  - Review proper usage of email system
  - Review process of releasing information, video, etc.
  - Review start of shift responsibilities - including equipment, CCTV inspection and checks
  - Review proper documentation of reporting and logging equipment, CCTV inspection and checks
  - Review how to complete daily paperwork - including daily logs, radio logs, key logs, etc.
  - Review how to properly document incidents - including reports, camera review, etc.
  - Review radio communication procedures, protocol and best practices
  - Review how to properly write reports and any computer generated report writing systems that may be utilized
  - Review proper telephone etiquette and how to handle emergency calls
  - Review the proper use of the Fire Command Center - including how to address alarms, the functionality of the system and how to conduct inspections of the equipment, etc.
  - Review of the types of alarms that report to the security surveillance center- including the proper response, when notifications are required, when emergency service, police, fire, etc., are to be advised to respond.
  - Review the emergency notification procedures - including what situations require notifications, who is to be notified, etc.
  - Review the process, procedure and protocol regarding the retention and coverage of incidents, accidents, investigations, etc.

The technological advances in the field of security surveillance centers are only limited to the imagination. However, there will always be a human element needed to perform and oversee the role and functions of the security surveillance center and the personnel responsible for the safety and security of all. An intricate part of this is the continual training of personnel, keeping abreast of best practices, training methods, training techniques, and the shifting sands of the legal aspects of security and surveillance.

In conclusion, it is important to continually self-educate in all areas of the security surveillance profession and in life. When knowledge is learned, it should be shared with members of the security surveillance center team and other professional organizations. Professionalism must translate into action. Only in this way will professionalism in the security surveillance field continue to grow locally and globally. This book was designed to shed light on areas that were unknown, unfamiliar, and to answer questions or concerns pertaining to establishing security surveillance centers. In crafting this book, it was my desire that readers would be able to gain clarification and knowledge in areas they were unacquainted with use this publication as a resource, and guide for training and establishing a new security surveillance center standard in the industry.

9 Test Questions

QUESTIONS

1. Elements that comprise the totality of circumstances approach include which of the following?
   a. Criminal incidents
   b. Location of incidents
   c. Nature of incidents
   d. Condition of property
   e. All of the above

2. What does the acronym CCTV stand for?
   a. Closed-circuit telecommunications
   b. Closed-circuitry telecommunications
   c. Closed-circuit television
   d. Cloistered-circuit television
   e. None of the above

3. Logs and documentation are designed to maintain an accurate record of actions, incidents, and reports.
   a. True
   b. False

4. What are the three levels of resolution obtained from a CCTV system?
   a. Covert, overt, and normal
   b. Identify, recognize, and plain view
   c. Clear, hazy, and moderate
   d. Detection, classification, and identification
   e. None of the above

5. What are the three types of keys properties generally use?
   a. Restricted, unrestricted, and company
   b. Small, medium, and large
   c. Electronic, hard, and soft
   d. Public, private, and property
   e. None of the above

6. How should entries be voided in a key log?
   a. Draw a single line through the entry
   b. Place initials next to the voided entry
   c. Make corrected entry on the next available line
   d. With red ink
   e. All of the above

7. Morality is
   a. Traditional customs or behavior
   b. Used to determine skill sets
   c. A measurement used to predict performance
   d. Answers a and b
   e. None of the above

8. When observing any area, security surveillance center personnel are looking for which of the following?
   a. Criminals
   b. Procedure violations
   c. Indications of violations of policy, procedure, and criminal activity
   d. Policy violations
   e. None of the above

9. What is the maximum number of monitors that a member of the security surveillance center should view?
   a. 10
   b. 12
   c. 16
   d. 18
   e. 33

10. In Frederick Herzberg's Hygiene Theory money is a motivator.
    a. True
    b. False

11. Which of the following is true regarding CCTV?
    a. CCTVs reduce the number of security personnel needed to monitor entrances and exits
    b. CCTVs are effective for control of personnel at entrances
    c. CCTVs can be used as a psychological deterrent
    d. CCTVs can be equipped with pan-tilt-zoom and digital recording features
    e. All of the above

12. People videotaped in a public area have no reasonable expectations of privacy.
    a. True
    b. False

13. An audit observation is a technique used to observe and monitor a specific person, area, activity, or department for an assigned period of time for the purpose of detecting violation of policy, procedure, theft, or fraud.
    a. True
    b. False

14. Why are best practices important to the operation of the security surveillance center?
    a. Provide maximum protection
    b. Provide detection of any activity or crisis that could impact a property
    c. Provide a safe environment
    d. Provide a secure environment
    e. All of the above

15. Which of the following are components of the fraud triangle?
    a. Motive, means, and support
    b. Pressure, opportunity, and support
    c. Opportunity, pressure, and rationalization
    d. Rationalization, opportunity, and means
    e. Pressure, motive, and rationalization

16. The lighting recommended for areas involving life and safety consideration in garages, parking lots, and other external locations should be at least
    a. 3 fc or lower
    b. 1 fc
    c. 5 fc and higher
    d. 2 fc
    e. 4 fc

17. Which of the following is the most important reason why the date of revision is placed on a revised policy or procedure?
    a. Indicates that a review or revision occurred
    b. Indicates the date of review or revision
    c. Is useful for legal and performance issues to determine what procedure was in effect at the time that an incident or accident occurred
    d. Is not useful for legal and performance issues
    e. None of the above

18. What are some ways to reduce eye fatigue of security surveillance center personnel?
    a. Reduce glare on monitors
    b. Direct face of monitor toward a darkened area in the room
    c. Do not have lighting reflect off of the front surface of the monitor
    d. Have operator regularly take a short break from viewing monitors
    e. All of the above

19. Who, what, when, where, why, and how should be answered in a report.
    a. True
    b. False

20. Which of the following is the main reason that the security surveillance center should conduct audits?
    a. To ensure policy and procedure are being adhered to
    b. To use as a scare tactic on employees to have them believe that the security surveillance center watches everything they do
    c. To justify the existence of the security surveillance center and its personnel
    d. All of the above
    e. None of the above

21. The three basic elements needed for fire are known as:
    a. The big three
    b. The fire triangle
    c. The tri-elements
    d. The fire cube
    e. None of the above

22. Values are:
    a. Provide direction in determining right from wrong
    b. Provide direction in determining good from bad
    c. Are what a person believes to have worth or importance
    d. All of the above
    e. None of the above

23. Which of the following CCTV assessment views provides the ability to describe a subject in detail?
    a. Detection
    b. Recognition
    c. Classification
    d. Identification
    e. Answers b and d

24. Which of the following would indicate possible theft or fraud in a restaurant or bar?
    a. Frequent cash overages
    b. Cashier-approved voids
    c. Cashier counting down register drawer during shift
    d. None of the above
    e. All of the above

25. Why should color be used sparingly in a security surveillance center?
    a. It creates a sense of playfulness
    b. Approximately 10% of the population has some form of color blindness
    c. It is a distraction
    d. It increases eye fatigue
    e. It is not cost efficient

26. What are the stages of fire?
    a. Incipient stage
    b. Smoldering stage
    c. Flammable stage
    d. Heat stage
    e. All of the above

27. What three things should be considered when determining monitor setups and displays within the security surveillance center?
    a. Location, room design, local regulations
    b. Property needs, informational flow, and past experience
    c. Leadership directives, room design, personnel input
    d. Revenue generated and local regulations
    e. None of the above

28. Do employees in positions of trust ever steal from the company they work for?
    a. Yes
    b. No

29. Why is ergonomics important in the design of a security surveillance center?
    a. Improves operator's effectiveness
    b. Reduces frustration
    c. Reduces fatigue
    d. Makes it easier to use equipment
    e. All of the above

30. CCTV cameras utilized by the security surveillance center should be left in their "at-rest" position when not in use by the operators.
    a. True
    b. False

31. The principles of using CCTV to monitor and record in public settings include which of the following?
    a. Identifying and gathering evidence
    b. Preventing employee misconduct
    c. Enhancing employee and guest safety
    d. Deterring employee misconduct
    e. All of the above

32. What are the most important reasons that time synchronization is important?
    a. Important for break schedules
    b. Crucial when reports of various systems are gathered for investigations, court, legal presentations, etc.
    c. Lets you know when people are late for work
    d. Ensures that overtime does not occur
    e. None of the above

33. Which of the following reasons explain why the restaurant and bar industry is vulnerable to fraud and theft?
    a. Inventory is untraceable
    b. Inventory is highly moveable
    c. Inventory is easily hidden
    d. All of the above
    e. Answers a and b

34. How often should procedures be reviewed and/or updated?
    a. Every 10 years
    b. At least every 6 to 12 months
    c. Every 3 years
    d. Every 5 years
    e. Never

35. Overt CCTV cameras help to provide a psychological deterrence in the protection of a property.
    a. True
    b. False

36. Which of the following does not have a legal impact on security surveillance centers?
    a. The Fourth Amendment
    b. *Katz v. United States*
    c. *United States v. Sawasky*
    d. *United States v. Knotts*
    e. All of the above

37. Foreseeability is the reasonable expectation that injury or harm is a likely result of an act or failure to act.
    a. True
    b. False

38. What is included in the Fourth Amendment?
    a. The right of people to be secure in their persons, houses, papers, and effects against unreasonable searches and seizures
    b. No warrants shall be issued, but upon probable cause
    c. No warrants shall be issued unless supported by oath or affirmation
    d. Warrants need to describe place to be searched, and the persons or things to be seized
    e. All of the above

39. According to the latest best practices, laws, and trends, a covert camera may be placed in which of the following areas?
    a. In a guest room
    b. Wherever it is deemed necessary to protect the property

    c. In locations where there is no reasonable expectation of privacy
    d. In a restroom
    e. Answers a and d

40. What significance does the United States Supreme Court case of *Katz v. United States* 389 U.S. 347 (1967) have in regard to CCTV and the Fourth Amendment?
    a. Does not have any significance
    b. Pertains to animal rights
    c. A person standing in a public park or walking along a public sidewalk cannot reasonably expect that this activity will be immune from the public eye or from observation by the police
    d. What a person seeks to preserve as private, even in an area accessible to the public, may be constitutionally protected
    e. Answers c and d

41. What does the acronym JDLR stand for?
    a. Just Do Like Right
    b. Just Doesn't Look Real
    c. Just Didn't Look Realistic
    d. Just Doesn't Look Right
    e. Just Did Look Real

42. What are the three main reasons the security surveillance center uses CCTV?
    a. Watch employees, watch guests, and watch visitors
    b. Witness what is happening, record what has happened, and act as a deterrent
    c. Create sense of well-being, protect public and records activity
    d. Use for court cases, use for criminal cases, and monitor activity of suspicious persons
    e. Use to identify visitors, track people entering property, and protect public

43. What are the three components used by security surveillance center personnel when the IOU patrol technique is utilized?
    a. Identify, observe, and understand
    b. Interview, obtain, and utilize
    c. Identify, obtain, and understand
    d. Intervene, outreach, and understand
    e. None of the above

44. Warehouse and receiving dock employees normally weigh meat, poultry, or seafood when it is delivered to verify that the shipment is accurate.
    a. True
    b. False

45. The security surveillance center can withstand legal scrutiny providing the operation of the program abides by which of the following?
    a. Focus cameras on guest areas
    b. Focus cameras on employee areas
    c. Follows proper procedures, protocol, best practices, and the law when disseminating images obtained
    d. Comply with all local, state, and federal case law regarding the use of surveillance cameras in employee and guest areas
    e. All of the above

46. Prior to moving on to another area to observe, security surveillance center personnel should do which of the following before classifying the area currently being observed as normal.
    a. Announce
    b. Understand
    c. Litigate
    d. Procrastinate
    e. Linger

47. In Frederick Herzberg's Hygiene Theory, which of the following are motivators?
    a. Achievement
    b. Recognition
    c. Responsibility
    d. Satisfaction from work
    e. All of the above

48. Which of the following US Supreme Court cases are relevant to CCTV and the Fourth Amendment?
    a. *United States v. Knotts*
    b. *Parker v. United States*
    c. *Oriti v. United States*
    d. *Katz v. United States*
    e. Both a and d

49. In Douglas McGregor's Theory X and Theory Y, the characteristics that make up Theory Y includes which of the following?
    a. People are creative
    b. People have the capacity for creativity
    c. Work can be as natural as play
    d. People usually seek and accept responsibility
    e. All of the above

50. What is an intentional tort?
    a. Probable cause
    b. Foreseeability that a crime will occur
    c. Circumstantial evidence

    d. Legal action where a wrong is committed against a person
    e. None of the above

51. What are the three categories of fraud that may require assistance from the security surveillance center?
    a. Fraudulent statements, asset misappropriation, and corruption
    b. Stealing inventory, payroll schemes, and billing schemes
    c. Theft, concealment, and corruption
    d. Billing schemes, cash schemes, payroll schemes
    e. None of the above

52. Why should the original unrevised copy of a procedure that has been revised be kept?
    a. For legal reasons
    b. To determine what procedure was in effect at the time that an accident occurred
    c. Performance issues
    d. To determine what procedure was in effect at the time that an incident occurred
    e. All of the above

53. The camera positioning of a point of sale should view the working area.
    a. True
    b. False

54. A mantrap is which of the following?
    a. Will only allow a door leading into a room to open after the outer door and all other doors are closed that are connected to that room
    b. A term used to detect IT sabotage
    c. A code name used for a sting operation
    d. Will always allow a door leading into a room to open as long as all the doors leading to and connected to the room are open
    e. None of the above

55. The three-step security surveillance center camera patrol technique—the IOU patrol method—is designed to conduct which of the following?
    a. Provide necessary evidence
    b. Proactively locate illicit activities
    c. Identify suspects
    d. All of the above
    e. None of the above

56. When items are received at the warehouse, packing materials are referred to as tare weight. The net weight equals the gross weight minus the tare weight.
    a. True
    b. False

57. What is the foreseeability approach?
   a. The belief that a person with ordinary intelligence should have foreseen
       the impact of an action or scenario that would have put himself or her-
       self or others in peril.
   b. That a person should have foreseen an incident before it occurred.
   c. The approach of operators to foresee events by the use of CCTV.
   d. When an event occurs that a reasonable person of average intelligence
       should have foreseen that their negligent act would put others or them-
       selves in danger.
   e. Both a and d

58. Which of the following are the main reasons to use CCTV in a security
    surveillance center?
   a. To witness what is happening
   b. To record what is happening
   c. Acts as a deterrent
   d. All of the above
   e. None of the above

59. Generally throughout the nation, what group has the largest negative impact
    on a company's bottom line?
   a. Shoplifters
   b. Organized crime
   c. Employees
   d. Outsiders
   e. None of the above

60. Tri-shot coverage is a basic camera setup used for monitoring an individual
    or area that is used for which of the following?
   a. Observation
   b. Investigation
   c. Evidence gathering
   d. All of the above
   e. None of the above

61. To protect against theft, which of the following safeguards should employees
    who receive meat and seafood products at the warehouse implement?
   a. Make sure products are delivered by the end of the day
   b. Weigh individually—do not weigh with other products or items
   c. Test the products
   d. Have delivery person stand by until product is delivered to outlet location
   e. None of the above

62. Which of the following are major elements of professionalism?
   a. Code of ethics
   b. Philosophy

c. Knowledge
d. Guidelines and standardization of job performance
e. All of the above

63. The security surveillance center must limit its use of CCTV to ensure that it does not violate the reasonable expectation of privacy as defined by the law?
a. True
b. False

64. Which of the following CCTV levels of assessment provide the most detail to the viewer?
a. Identification
b. Recognition
c. Classification
d. Detection
e. Answers b and c

65. To protect against theft, when checking delivered products, employees who receive the products should be on the lookout for excess ice, watered-down product, and other packaging that can add dead weight.
a. True
b. False

66. Which of the following should be considered when designing a security surveillance center?
a. What are the specific needs of the facility?
b. What are the expectations from leadership?
c. What are the job duties personnel in this area are expected to perform?
d. All of the above
e. None of the above

67. What does the acronym IOU stand for?
a. Intention, obligation, and utilization
b. Identify, observe, and understand
c. Incident, occurrence, and usefulness
d. Both a and c
e. None of the above

68. Which of the following addresses the importance of the plain view rule and open field doctrine as it relates to the operation of the security surveillance center?
a. People videotaped in a public area have no reasonable expectations of privacy and this therefore does not violate the Fourth Amendment.
b. Transactions in plain view in a public area generally raise Fourth Amendment concerns.

    c. Transactions in plain view in a public area generally do not raise Fourth Amendment concerns.

    d. Both a and c

    e. People videotaped in a public area have a reasonable expectation of privacy; therefore, this violates the Fourth Amendment.

69. An employer is vicariously liable for the actions of an employee when which of the following occurs?

    a. When the employee has a good attorney

    b. The employee is acting within the scope of his or her employment

    c. When the employee feels the employer is liable

    d. If the employee directly violates written procedures

    e. Answers a and c

70. An open-door policy provides a conduit to facilitate good communications between all members of the security surveillance center.

    a. True

    b. False

71. What does the acronym PTZ stand for?

    a. Pass-turn-zoom

    b. Pan-tilt-zoom

    c. Play-toss-zoom

    d. Prevent-terminate-zoom

    e. None of the above

72. An audit is an observation technique used to observe a specific person, area, activity, or department for an assigned period of time with the purpose of which of the following?

    a. Detecting violation of policy

    b. Detecting theft

    c. Detecting violation of procedure

    d. Detecting fraud

    e. All of the above

73. Which of the following may be a reason an employee may steal from his or her employer?

    a. Disgruntled

    b. Alcohol and/or drug abuse problems

    c. Excessive gambling debts

    d. Living above one's means

    e. All of the above

74. The security surveillance center may place cameras in bathrooms and changing rooms, where there is an expectation of privacy.

    a. True

    b. False

75. Which of the following areas should be included when deciding on the best camera coverage to protect guests, patrons, and employees?
    a. Entrances
    b. Exits
    c. Thoroughfares
    d. Back of house areas
    e. All of the above

76. When setting up camera coverage of personnel responding to an incident, a best practice is to keep a wide shot of the incident to provide coverage of the response to the situation.
    a. True
    b. False

77. In what manner should the security surveillance center conduct the monitoring and recording of others?
    a. In a professional manner
    b. In an ethical manner
    c. In a legal manner
    d. In a diligent manner
    e. All of the above

78. Which of the following CCTV assessment views provides sthe ability to classify an object into a class i.e., animal, human, vehicle, etc.?
    a. Detection
    b. Recognition
    c. Magnification
    d. Identification
    e. Answers b and c

79. What are the primary responsibilities of security surveillance center personnel?
    a. Observe
    b. Document
    c. Notify
    d. All of the above
    e. None of the above

80. Which of the following should be implemented to reduce embezzlement committed by cashiers?
    a. Drug testing
    b. Institute a variance policy where variance investigations are conducted by security surveillance center personnel above a certain dollar amount.
    c. Report variance to law enforcement.
    d. None of the above
    e. All of the above

81. Security surveillance center personnel should check which of the following components of the CCTV video equipment daily to ensure that it is working properly?
    a. Recording
    b. Time stamp
    c. Playback
    d. Live views
    e. All of the above

82. The comingling of funds is when a cashier co-mingles funds from a cash register with personal funds and pockets them. This act is known as embezzlement.
    a. True
    b. False

83. The acronym ROI is an abbreviation for which of the following?
    a. Return On Investment
    b. Relie On Intuition
    c. Relay Only Information
    d. Resources On Intelligence
    e. Recently On Investigation

84. The proper control of evidence should include which of the following?
    a. An assigned evidence custodian
    b. A secured storage area
    c. Documentation of the chain of custody
    d. All of the above
    e. None of the above

85. Which of the following are the positive results of an effective setup and display?
    a. Proactive operations
    b. Timely response with minimum effort
    c. Maximum deterrence
    d. Identification of suspects
    e. All of the above

86. What are the three basic elements needed for fire?
    a. H_2O, flame, and heat
    b. Oxygen, heat, and fuel
    c. Carbon dioxide, heat, and fuel
    d. Oxygen, flames, and carbon
    e. None of the above

87. Ethics is
    a. About right or wrong
    b. About benefit and harm

    c. About vice and virtue

    d. The way morals are practiced

    e. All of the above

88. When "burning" a CCTV disk of an incident for a case, it is a best practice to place at least 5 minutes preceding the incident and 5 minutes after the incident has concluded on the disk.
    a. True
    b. False

89. The Imminent Threat alert from the National Terrorism Advisory System (NTAS) warns of
    a. A credible terrorist threat against the United States
    b. A specific terrorist threat against the United States
    c. An impending terrorist threat against the United States
    d. A specific terrorist threat against Europe
    e. Answers a, b, and c

90. Points of sale (POSs) should have CCTV camera coverage?
    a. True
    b. False

91. In Frederick Herzberg's Hygiene Theory, hygiene factors can move someone from dissatisfaction to satisfaction.
    a. True
    b. False

92. Information obtained through video surveillance should be treated as confidential.
    a. True
    b. False

93. The Elevated Threat alert from the National Terrorism Advisory System (NTAS) warns of
    a. An incredible terrorist threat against the United Kingdom
    b. A credible terrorist threat against Europe
    c. A credible terrorist threat against the United States
    d. Answers a and c
    e. All of the above

94. Security surveillance center leaders and personnel should be trained in the legal issues involved in video surveillance.
    a. True
    b. False

95. Which of the following is a fire watch?
    a. The action of an on-site person whose sole responsibility is to watch for the occurrence of fire
    b. A person who watches an active fire
    c. Documentation of the arrival and actions of personnel who respond to an active fire
    d. The person who has the responsibility of watching first responders extinguish an active fire
    e. None of the above

96. Which of the following should be considered prior to selecting systems or products for the security surveillance center?
    a. The life cycle
    b. When potential upgrades or changes are expected to occur
    c. Maintenance cycle
    d. All of the above
    e. None of the above

97. In Frederick Herzberg's Hygiene Theory, which of the following are examples of hygiene factors that can move someone from dissatisfaction to no satisfaction?
    a. Surroundings
    b. Salary
    c. External factors
    d. Motivation factors
    e. All of the above

98. When writing a report, which of the following should be done?
    a. Provide opinion
    b. Report the facts
    c. Speculate
    d. Report hearsay
    e. Answers a, c, and d

99. Security surveillance center personnel should reveal all information discovered during the course of an investigation or during the performance of their duties, which if omitted, could cause distortion of the facts.
    a. True
    b. False

100. Which of the following are the benefits of conducting IOU patrols?
    a. Provide consistent detection of illicit activity
    b. Provide a constant flow of information
    c. Provide a proactive, systematic, and thorough method of patrol
    d. Provide information for investigative purposes
    e. All of the above

ANSWERS

1. e. All of the above
2. c. Closed-circuit television
3. a. True
4. d. Detection, classification, and identification
5. a. Restricted, unrestricted, and company
6. e. All of the above
7. a. Traditional customs or behavior
8. c. Indications of violations of policy, procedure, and criminal activity
9. c. 16
10. b. False
11. e. All of the above
12. a. True
13. a. True
14. e. All of the above
15. c. Opportunity, pressure, and rationalization
16. c. 5 fc and higher
17. c. Is useful for legal and performance issues to determine what procedure was in effect at the time that an incident or accident occurred
18. e. All of the above
19. a. True
20. a. To ensure policy and procedure are being adhered to
21. b. The fire triangle
22. d. All of the above
23. d. Identification
24. e. All of the above
25. b. Approximately 10% of the population has some form of color blindness.
26. e. All of the above
27. b. Property needs, informational flow, and past experience
28. a. Yes
29. e. All of the above
30. a. True
31. e. All of the above
32. b. Crucial when reports of various systems are gathered for investigations, court, legal presentations, and so on
33. d. All of the above
34. b. At least every 6 to 12 months
35. a. True
36. c. *United States v. Sawasky*
37. a. True
38. e. All of the above
39. c. In locations where there is no reasonable expectation of privacy
40. e. Answers c and d
41. d. Just Doesn't Look Right
42. b. Witness what is happening, record what has happened, and act as a deterrent

43. a. Identify, observe, and understand
44. a. True
45. e. All of the above
46. b. Understand
47. e. All of the above
48. e. Both a and d
49. e. All of the above
50. d. Legal action where a wrong is committed against a person
51. a. Fraudulent statements, asset misappropriation, and corruption
52. e. All of the above
53. a. True
54. a. Will only allow a door leading into a room to open after the outer door and all other doors are closed that are connected to that room
55. d. All of the above
56. a. True
57. e. Both a and d
58. d. All of the above
59. c. Employees
60. d. All of the above
61. b. Weigh individually—do not weigh with other products or items
62. e. All of the above
63. a. True
64. a. Identification
65. a. True
66. d. All of the above
67. b. Identify, Observe, and Understand
68. d. Both a and c
69. b. The employee is acting within the scope of his or her employment
70. a. True
71. b. Pan-tilt-zoom
72. e. All of the above
73. e. All of the above
74. b. False
75. e. All of the above
76. a. True
77. e. All of the above
78. b. Recognition
79. d. All of the above
80. b. Institute a variance policy where variance investigations are conducted by security surveillance center personnel above a certain dollar amount.
81. e. All of the above
82. a. True
83. a. Return On Investment
84. d. All of the above
85. e. All of the above
86. b. Oxygen, heat, and fuel

87. e. All of the above
88. a. True
89. e. Answers a, b, and c
90. a. True
91. b. False
92. a. True
93. c. A credible terrorist threat against the United States
94. a. True
95. a. The action of an on-site person whose sole responsibility is to watch for the occurrence of fire
96. d. All of the above
97. e. All of the above
98. b. Report the facts
99. a. True
100. e. All of the above

Glossary

AC Adaptor: The AC adaptor converts the AC power to DC power and will adjust it to a specified amperage.

Activity Detection: Multiplexers use this video motion detection technique that improves the ability to save data for a longer period of time by not recording all of the time. Will only record when there is activity or motion in the field of view of the camera.

AES (Auto Electronic Shutter): The ability of the camera to compensate for moderate light changes without the use of an auto-iris lens.

Affidavit: A written declaration or statement of facts, made under oath or magistrate before an officer having authority to administer oaths.

Alarm Input: A connection from an alarm or sensor that, when activated, triggers the CCTV unit to start recording, generate an audible alert, send an email, etc.

Alarm Malfunction: An alarm signal that is received without the presence of an alarm condition. Also known as a false alarm. This can be caused by many factors including rain, fog, wind, lighting, temperature changes, animals, insects, equipment malfunctions, operator error, and so on.

Angle of View: This refers to the angular range in degrees that you can focus the camera without distorting the image. The larger the angle of view, the individual object will appears smaller in the image.

Aperture: The opening of a lens that controls the amount of light permitted into the camera. The wider the aperture, the more light will pass through.

Armor Dome: Refers to a high-impact reinforced polycarbonate dome casing designed to resist vandalism and tampering.

Audible Alarm Device: A noise-making device used as part of an alarm system to indicate an alarm condition. These devices provide an audible, visual or other form of alarm signal which includes sirens, bells, horns, etc,. This can also be used as part of an annunciator to indicate a change in the status or operating mode of an alarm system.

Audit: Security surveillance center assignment to personnel to detect a violation of controls, policies, procedures, theft, or fraud, requiring observation of an area, transaction, department, or employee(s).

Auto Electronic Shutter: Allows the camera to compensate for moderate light changes in indoor applications without the use of auto-iris lenses.

Auto-Iris Lens: The iris is controlled automatically to regulate the amount of light entering the camera, to maintain proper light levels throughout varying light conditions.

Automatic Brightness Control: Automatically, the light level of a monitor or video image from a camera controls brightness.

Baud: The speed at which data are transmitted (i.e., 1 baud = 1 bit per second).

Bill of Rights: The first 10 amendments of the United States Constitution.

Biometrics: Biometrics is the technology and science of authenticating individuals by measuring their physiological or behavioral features.

Blooming: The defocusing of regions of the picture where the brightness is at an excessive level to part of the image.

BNC Connector: Type of connector that interconnects two coaxial cables or connects a cable with CCTV components—commonly used for CCTV installations.

Bullet Camera: A type of camera with a bullet-like shape.

Camera Housing: An enclosure designed to protect video cameras from weather exposure when placed outdoors to protect from tampering or theft.

CAT5 (Category 5): Type of cable most often used in networking applications.

CCTV (Closed-Circuit Television): Captures a scene image and converts to a display or recording device consists of cameras, recording and monitoring equipment over a dedicated cabling or transmission system.

CCTV Monitor: Receives and displays the picture from the CCTV camera.

Central Station: An alarm systems control center in a subscriber's premises is connected, circuits are supervised, and where personnel are positioned continuously to record and investigate alarm or trouble signals. Facilities are provided for the reporting of alarms to police, fire departments, or other outside agencies.

Central Station Alarm System: An alarm system that transmits the alarm signal to the central station. This differs from a proprietary alarm in that the central station is owned and operated independently of the subscriber.

Close Watch: Usually initiated by a tip. A surveillance observation of an area or subject requiring continuous monitoring by the surveillance center.

Coaxial Cable: A particular type of cable capable of passing a wide range of frequencies with very low signal loss—RG59 is a commonly used coaxial cable used for CCTV installations. Basically, it is a stranded metallic shield with a single wire placed along the center of the shield, which is isolated from the shield by an insulator.

Compressed Picture: A full-size picture that has been reduced in size while still displaying all of the original screen information.

Compression: Compression occurs when an incoming signal or image takes fewer resources for storage and transmission.

Conductor: Material with the ability to carry electric current.

Contrast: The range or difference of light to dark values in a picture.

Coverage: For the purposes of a security surveillance center, coverage refers to the video of an incident taken from the cameras recording.

Covert: When cameras are used in a manner where they are hidden and the use is unknown to those being watched or recorded.

Covert Surveillance: The use of hidden cameras to observe a scene without being seen.

Day/Night Camera: Regular cameras with a highly sensitive CCD chip with the ability to capture quality imagery with very little light.

DC (Direct Current): Electricity always flows through it in the same direction. A pair of wires has one positive wire and one negative.

Detection: Observation of a crime, policy, or procedure violation.

Dome Camera: Camera with a dome-like shape.

Duplex: Ability to transfer data in and out of the recorder at the same time. For example, is capable of both playback and recording at the same time.

DVR (Digital Video Recorder): Converts the incoming (analog) signal from cameras to digital, and compresses and stores the data.

Dwell Time: The time a multiplexer or DVR displays one camera before moving to the next one in the sequence.

Factory Default Settings: Settings originally applied to a device by the factory.

Fail-Safe: A feature of a system or device that initiates an alarm or trouble signal when the system or device either malfunctions or loses power. For example, doors that are normally locked will unlock in the event of a fail-safe condition.

Fail Secure: A feature of a system or device that initiates an alarm or trouble signal when the system or device either malfunctions or loses power. For example, doors will lock in the event of a fail-secure condition. A setting where this would occur is in a prison environment.

False Alarm: An alarm signal that is received without the presence of an alarm condition. Also known as an alarm malfunction. This can be caused by many factors including rain, fog, wind, lighting, temperature changes, animals, insects, equipment malfunctions, operator error, and so on.

False Imprisonment: The unlawful restraint by a person of another.

Fence Disturbance Sensor: The perimeter fence around a site may have one of these installed around it for intrusion detection. These sensors can be interfaced with a CCTV switcher so that specific cameras are activated in an area where the disturbance is detected.

Field of View: The angle of view that can be seen through a lens.

Firewall: A firewall is a software or hardware application utilized to prevent unauthorized users from accessing a computer. A firewall works as a barrier between networks and ensures that only authorized users are granted access.

F-Number: Indicates the brightness of the image formed by the lens, controlled by the iris. The smaller the F-number, the brighter the image.

Focal Length: The distance from the focal point to the principle point of the lens. Lower lengths give a greater field of view and less magnification. Longer lengths give a narrower field of view and greater magnification.

Foreseeability: Element of proximate cause in a tort claim. Should have been able to see that an event could happen.

FPS (Frames per Second): Refers to the number of video images that can be captured, displayed, or recorded in a second. Thirty frames per second or more results in playback looking like real time, without hesitation or broken movements in the video.

Frame Frequency: The number of times per second that a frame is scanned. The US standard is 30 frames per second.

Frame Rate: The number of frames per second that the camera produces. The US standard frame time is 1/30 second.

Fraud: Theft by deception.

Frederick Herzberg's Hygiene Theory: States opposite of satisfaction is not dissatisfaction, but rather no satisfaction. Hygiene factors can move someone from dissatisfaction to no satisfaction. Only motivators can move someone to satisfaction.

F-Stop: Indicates the speed of a lens. The greater amount of light that passes through the lens, the smaller the F-number will be.

Ghost: A spurious image resulting from an echo. This is when an image moves across a computer screen leaving a brief lingering shadow of itself where it had just been, leaving a "ghost" image. This is often caused by badly transmitted coaxial cables.

Hardwired: Direct connection between one product and another, used for control of equipment in simple systems.

Holdup Alarm System, Manual: A holdup alarm system in which the signal transmission is initiated by the direct action of the individual attacked or of an observer of an attack.

Holdup button: A manually activated mechanical switch used to initiate a duress alarm signal. Usually located and constructed in a manner to minimize accidental activation.

Housing: A covering or container designed to protect cameras from the weather.

Hub: Network device that enables attached devices to receive data that are transmitted over a network and interconnects with clients and servers.

Infrared Camera: Captures good images in total darkness due to special infrared lights installed around the outside of the camera lens.

Infrared Detector: This is an alarm that uses infrared light to detect nearby movement.

Insider: A person who has knowledge of a facilities operation and physical security system by reason of his or her official duties. This person is in a position to significantly enhance the likelihood of successful bypass of or defeating of the security surveillance measures of the facility.

IOU: Security surveillance center acronym for a patrol technique: identify, observe, understand.

IOU Patrol: Security surveillance technique used to determine if an activity is a threat. Also used to gather evidence.

IP Address: An IP address is the unique address of a computer or network device connected to that network. IP addresses allow network computers and devices to locate each other and transfer data back and forth. An IP address is required for positive unique identification of any device on a network or the Internet.

IP Camera: An IP camera (or network camera) captures and transmits live video images directly over an IP network. Each camera has a built-in Web server and its own IP address.

Iris: An adjustable aperture built into a camera lens to control the amount of light passing through the lens.

Jamming: An intruder's attempt to prevent radio communications through destruction of communications equipment or by inserting unwanted signals into the frequency channel of the communications system.

Joystick: Used to control a PTZ security camera's pan and tilt head.

JPEG (Joint Photographic Experts Group): This is a standard way of compressing photographic images. JPEG is a standard for the encoding and compression of images, which works well for photographic and still images.

LAN (Local Area Network): A high-speed network connecting computers that are in relatively close proximity to one allow the sharing of resources and data.

Local Alarm: When activated makes a loud noise and/or floods the area with lights at or near the protected area.

Local Alarm System: When activated produces audible or visual signals in the immediate location of the protected area or object.

Loss Prevention: The practice of securing devices or information from theft or loss. Video surveillance is a common practice in preventing theft or other types of losses.

Luminance: Refers to the part of a video signal that carries the monochrome information-brightness information.

Lux: The amount of light required for a camera to capture a good image.

Manual Iris Lens: A lens with a manual adjustment to set the iris opening (F-stop) to a specific position.

Matrix Switch: The routing of signal sources. For example, in video cameras they are switched to monitors, recorders, and networks.

McGregor Theory X and Theory Y: Theory based on the type of people X and Y. Characteristics of that make up those categories:
    X: not ambitious, resist change, avoid work, prefer to be directed.
    Y: creative, work can be as nature as play, ingenuity is common.

Megapixel IP Camera: Provides high image detail, has a broader field of view than a conventional camera, and allows users to zoom in on specific portions of a scene without a significant loss in image detail.

Monitor: Displays the images captured by cameras; data from computer systems and other visual information.

Motion Detection: The recording and automated alerts occur only when motion is perceived. This helps to optimize bandwidth and preserve storage space. Predefined motion detection zones and sensitivity for each individual camera allows for space to be saved on the hard drive by only recording relevant events triggered by motion.

Motion Detector: A sensor that responds to motion and generates an alarm.

MPEG (Moving Pictures Expert Group): An international group that set standards for audio and video compression.

Multiplexer: A device that can accept a number of camera inputs and simultaneously display and record them.

Multiplexing: A technique for the concurrent transmission of two or more signals in either or both directions over the same wire, carrier, or other communication channel.

Network: A collection of devices that are connected together so that information and resources can be shared. These include computers, storage devices, printers, etc.

Network Camera: Captures and streams live video images directly over an IP network.

Nuisance Alarm: Any alarm that is not caused by an intrusion. Also referred to as a false alarm or alarm malfunction.

NVR (Network Video Recorder): Accepts IP camera inputs. NVRs can be software based, making them suitable for accepting IP camera streams over the Internet.

Object Protection: Protection of objects such as files, safes, or anything of value that could be damaged or removed from a facility.

Observe: The basic function of a security surveillance center—observe and report. The surveillance of a person or an area. Also referred to as monitoring.

Outdoor Camera: Cameras that are encased in special weatherproof housings that allow them to perform well in a wide range of weather and temperature conditions.

Outdoor Camera Housing: A protective shell for cameras used in outdoor conditions; they typically have cooling fans for hot weather use and heaters for cold weather use.

Pan–tilt–zoom (PTZ): The functions of mounted cameras that have the ability to be moved by a controller. The panning of the camera is the movement of the camera horizontally. The tilt of the camera is the movement of the camera vertically, and the zoom of the camera is the movement of the camera that magnifies the image.

Patrol: The movement of cameras of an activity or an area.

Phony Walkout: Cashier or server claims a customer left without paying, and the cashier or server keeps the money.

Photoelectric Alarm System: Uses a light beam and a photoelectric sensor to provide a line of protection. Any interruption to the light beam will be detected by the photoelectric sensor. Mirrors may be used in this system to change the direction of the beam.

Pixel: Refers to an individual area on the surface of the imaging device. It is made from photosensitive material that converts light into electrical energy.

Primary Colors: Colors where no mixture of two can make the third. In color television, the primary colors normally used are red (R), green (G), and blue (B).

Proprietary Alarm System: An alarm system similar to a central station alarm system except that the annunciator is owned and operated by the facility. The facility ensures that it is constantly maintained and monitored, and all alarm signals and alerts are responded to with notification to the proper authorities.

Protection of Assets: One of the main objectives of the security surveillance center.

PTZ Controller: The controller used to control PTZ camera movement, usually software or a joystick.

Quad: The simultaneous display of four cameras on a single monitor.

Real-Time Recording: 30 frames per second or more equals real time where there is no hesitation or broken movements in the video.

Resolution: The measure of how much detail an image can hold. The higher the resolution, the more detailed are the images.

Response: A security surveillance center reaction to an observation or threat that requires action.

RG-59: A coaxial cable used in CCTV applications.

Router: Facilitates the exchange of information throughout LAN or WAN networks. Bridges two or more networks.

Rubbernecking: The method criminals use to constantly look around to detect if anyone is watching them or is aware of their activities.

Server: A computer program that provides services to other computer programs.

Shield: A covering put between cables to prevent interference caused by signal leakage.

Shunt: A deliberate shorting out of a portion of an electric circuit allowing entry into a protected area without initiating an alarm signal.

Silent Alarm: A remote alarm activated without an audible alert such as bells, and horns, etc.

Spoofing: Any technique that allows for an intruder to pass through a sensor's detection zone without generating an alarm by tricking or fooling its detection system.

Supervisory Alarm System: Monitors conditions and signals for any deviation from an established norm.

Tampering Alarm: Detects when a camera is being tampered with and activates an alarm.

Telephoto Lens: Produces a narrow field of view, used to magnify objects within their viewing area.

Transformer: Used to transfer electric energy from one circuit to another.

Tri-Shot: A basic security surveillance center camera setup that is used to gather and provide the minimum information and evidence needed to determine who, what, when, where, and how.

Trouble Signal: Indicates trouble of any nature, including opening or breaking of an electrical circuit and possible system failure.

UPS (Uninterruptible Power Supply): Supplies power to a system without losing data and allows for the continued operation of a system for a specific time period during a power failure.

Varifocal Lens: A camera lens in which the focus is not fixed; it can be manually adjusted to provide a range of view.

Vibration Sensor: A device that activates when it detects vibrations in its detection zone, and then activates a specific surveillance camera.

Video Motion Detection: A system that detects motion in the video signal and generates a corresponding alarm. This feature maximizes recording space by only recording while motion is detected.

Waterproof: A device that can be immersed in water and still function properly.

Weatherproof: Can be installed outside and stand up to harsh weather conditions and temperatures. Weatherproof does not equal waterproof.

Wired Camera: A camera that transmits its signal via cable back to the recording/control device.

Wireless Camera: Wireless cameras allow transmissions to the receiver without having to run wires.

Wireless Network Camera: Connects to a network wirelessly allowing for flexible installation in virtually any location. Allows the transmission of data to a receiver without having to run wires.

Zoom: The ability to zero in on specific details; enables the size of the scene image to be enlarged or reduced.

Zoom Lens: Has the ability to change its focal length manually or through the use of a controller.

Z-Out: Closing out retail or food and beverage cash registers or point of sale (POS) to determine sales.

Forms

The following are examples that could be useful in the creation of forms for the operation of a security surveillance center. It is a best practice to have your legal department and the executive leadership team review and approve all forms prior to their usage. All forms that are utilized by the security surveillance center should be reviewed and updated, as needed, at least every 6–12 months to ensure that they are in compliance with all laws, ordinances, and legal trends in the jurisdiction where they are being used.

SECURITY SURVEILLANCE CENTER CAMERA CHECKLIST

Camera Number	Working Properly Yes or No	Issues Yes or No	Inspected by Name and ID #	Description of Issues
1				
2				
3				
4				
5				
6				
7				
8				
9				
10				
11				
12				
13				
14				
15				
16				
17				
18				
19				
20				
21				
22				
23				
24				
25				
26				
27				
28				
29				
30				
31				
32				
33				
34				
35				
36				
37				
38				
39				
40				
41				
42				
43				
44				
45				
46				
47				
48				
49				
50				

CAMERA LOG

CAMERA	LOCATION	TYPE (PTZ or FIXED)	COMMENTS
1			
2			
3			
4			
5			
6			
7			
8			
9			
10			
11			
12			
13			
14			
15			
16			
17			
18			
19			
20			
21			
22			
23			
24			
25			
26			
27			
28			
29			
30			
31			
32			
33			
34			
35			
36			
37			

SECURITY SURVEILLANCE CENTER EVIDENCE LOG

EVIDENCE#	DATE	REPORT#	INCIDENT—Person's Name (Last Name First) and Incident Type	NAME and ID#

SECURITY SURVEILLANCE CENTER
DIGITAL VIDEO RELEASE AUTHORIZATION

DATE: _____ TIME: _____

I _____
PRINT NAME

_____
SIGNATURE/EMPLOYEE #

AUTHORIZE THE RELEASE OF DIGITAL VIDEO EVIDENCE IN
REGARDS TO:

_____

TO: _____
PRINT NAME

SIGNATURE: _____

DEPARTMENT: _____

SECURITY SURVEILLANCE CENTER
RECEIPT

DATE: _____

REQUESTED BY: _____
(PRINT NAME AND EMPLOYEE BADGE NUMBER)

RELEASED TO: _____
(PRINT NAME AND EMPLOYEE BADGE NUMBER)

_____
(SIGNATURE & TITLE)

DESCRIPTION: _____

_____

_____

PURPOSE—PLEASE CIRCLE ONE OF THE FOLLOWING:

☐ EVIDENCE

☐ FOR SAFEKEEPING

RELEASED BY: _____
(PRINT NAME AND EMPLOYEE NUMBER)

_____
(SIGNATURE & TITLE)

SECURITY SURVEILLANCE CENTER
PHOTOGRAPH RELEASE FORM

Requested By: _____

_____

Reason for Request _____

_____

_____

_____

_____

_____

_____

_____

_____

Date of Incident: _____ Time of Incident: _____

Person Requesting (Print Name): _____ Department: _____

Signature _____

Security Surveillance Operator (Print Name): _____

Security Surveillance Operator Signature: _____

Date of Release: _____ Time of Release: _____

ACKNOWLEDGMENT

On behalf of the _____ Police Department, the undersigned acknowledges that the requested video(s)/DVD(s) are intended to be used solely in an ongoing criminal investigation or prosecution of a crime.

The below listed items being furnished by _____
[Name of Property] will be used only in accordance with this request for the Security Surveillance Center Video/DVD pursuant to a criminal investigation or prosecution of a crime that has been presented to _____
[Name of Property].

Video(s)/DVD(s) Being Furnished:

_____

_____

_____

_____

_____

_____

Dated this ____ day of _____, 20___

Released To:

Signature:_____

Printed Name:_____

Badge Number:_____

Date Received: _____

Released By: _____

Member of Security Surveillance Center Leadership Team
(Print Name and ID #)

_____

Signature of Member of Security Surveillance Center
Leadership Team

REQUEST FOR SECURITY SURVEILLANCE CENTER VIDEO/DVD PURSUANT TO A CRIMINAL INVESTIGATION

_____ POLICE DEPARTMENT

_____
(Insert Name of Establishment)

This request is being served to further a criminal investigation currently being conducted by the _____ Police Department. To accommodate the needs of law enforcement while minimizing the intrusion into the business from which this evidence is sought:

It is requested that a true and accurate copy of the following video(s)/DVD(s) to assist us in identifying a person of interest be produced:

I. Security Surveillance Center video/DVD, pertaining to: _____
    (Police Event or Report # _____ if applicable)

The request for video(s)/DVD(s) are requested for use in an ongoing criminal investigation and prosecution. The video(s)/DVD(s) received shall at all times be held by _____ Police Department solely as evidence and, shall not be released by _____ Police Department to any other person or entity except (a) as required by law or Court Order or to further the investigation which may include sharing portions with other law enforcement agencies for the purpose of assisting with the identification and/or apprehension of a criminal suspect. _____ Police Department shall return video(s)/DVD(s) to [_____ INSERT PROPERTY NAME], when it is no longer needed.

Please respond to this request on or before _____, 20___.

Any questions regarding this request please contact:

Officer/Detective: _____ Section/Bureau: _____

Phone #: _____ Fax #: _____

Email: _____ Dated: Day _____ Month _____, 20___.

Requested By:_____
(Print Name)

Requested By:_____
(Signature and Badge Number)

Bureau Commander or Designee, _____
(Insert Bureau Name)

Date Received: _____

Received By: _____

Member of Security Surveillance Center Leadership Team
(Print Name and ID #)

_____
Signature of Member of Security Surveillance Center Leadership Team

Security Surveillance Center Internal Loss Investigations Log

Incident Date	Department	Employee Name	Location	Variance Shortage	Variance Overage	Completion Date	Time	Security Surveillance Center Personnel

SECURITY SURVEILLANCE CENTER
SPECIAL REPORT

EMPLOYEE NAME: DATES: EMPLOYEE ID NUMBER:

Time	Camera Location Name/Number	Details

SECURITY SURVEILLANCE CENTER ALARM CHECKLIST

LOCATION	DATE	TIME	ALARM WORKING		RESPONDER	COMMENTS	TIME ALARM ACTIVATED	TIME ALARM RESET
			YES	NO				

Print Name and Identification #: _____

Signature: _____

ELEVATOR EMERGENCY BUTTONS AND CAMERA CHECKLIST

Elevator Call Button	Working	Not Working	Comments
	Yes or No	Yes or No	
Elevator 1			
Elevator 2			
Elevator 3			
Elevator 4			
Elevator 5			
Elevator 6			
Elevator 7			
Elevator 8			
Elevator 9			
Elevator 10			
Elevator 11			
Elevator 12			
Elevator 13			
Elevator 14			
Elevator 15			
Elevator 16			
Elevator 17			
Elevator 18			
Elevator 19			
Elevator 20			
Elevator 21			
Elevator 22			
Elevator 23			
Elevator 24			
Elevator 25			
Elevator 26			

Name and ID # _____

Date _____

Time _____

Signature _____

SECURITY SURVEILLANCE CENTER
EMERGENCY BOX AND CAMERA CHECKLIST

Box #	Working	Not Working	Camera #	Comments
Level 1	Yes or No	Yes or No		
Box #	Working	Not Working	Camera #	
Level 2	Yes or No	Yes or No		
Box #	Working	Not Working	Camera #	
Level 3	Yes or No	Yes or No		
Box #	Working	Not Working	Camera #	
Level 4	Yes or No	Yes or No		
Box #	Working	Not Working	Camera #	
Level 5	Yes or No	Yes or No		
Box #	Working	Not Working	Camera #	
Level 6	Yes or No	Yes or No		
Box #	Working	Not Working	Camera #	
Level 7	Yes or No	Yes or No		
Box #	Working	Not Working	Camera #	
Level 8	Yes or No	Yes or No		

Name _____

Date _____

Time _____

Signature _____

SECURITY SURVEILLANCE CENTER EMERGENCY KEY LOG

Date and Time Out	Key #	Reason for key	Name and #	Signature Out	Date and Time IN	Signature IN	Security Surveillance Center Personnel Name Out	Security Surveillance Center Personnel Name In

SECURITY SURVEILLANCE CENTER ENTRY LOG

DATE: _____   DAY: _____

TIME IN	TIME OUT	PERSON'S NAME	AGENCY/DEPARTMENT	REASON

FLASHLIGHT SIGN OUT SHEET

FLASHLIGHT #		PRINT NAME		FLASHLIGHT #		PRINT NAME
1				21		
2				22		
3				23		
4				24		
5				25		
6				26		
7				27		
8				28		
9				29		
10				30		
11				31		
12				32		
13				33		
14				34		
15				35		
16				36		
17				37		
18				38		
19				39		
20				40		

Security Surveillance Center Leader Name and ID #: _____

SECURITY SURVEILLANCE CENTER VIDEO REVIEW LOG

Date	Time	Person being reviewed	Department	Incident Information	Security Surveillance Center Representative

SECURITY SURVEILLANCE CENTER
CHAIN OF CUSTODY FORM

Date and Time: _____   Incident Type: _____   Incident Report #: _____

Item #   Quantity   Description

_____   _____   _____

_____   _____   _____

_____   _____   _____

The above represents all items taken from my possession.

_____

Print Name and Signature

I acknowledge that the above represents all items taken and retained as evidence.

_____

Security Surveillance Center Representative - Print Name - Identification
Number and Signature

Security Surveillance Center Leader Releasing Item(s):

_____

Print Name - Identification Number and Signature

Reason Released: _____   Released To: _____
Date Released: _____   Time Released: _____
Returned By: _____   Date & Time Returned: _____

Security Surveillance Center Leader Returning Item(s) to Evidence:

_____

Print Name - Identification Number and Signature

Security Surveillance Center Leader Releasing Item(s):

_____

Print Name - Identification Number and Signature

Reason Released: _____   Released To: _____
Date Released: _____   Time Released: _____
Returned By: _____   Date & Time Returned: _____

Security Surveillance Center Leader Returning Item(s) to Evidence:

_____

Print Name - Identification Number and Signature

Index

For Product Safety Concerns and Information please contact our EU
representative GPSR@taylorandfrancis.com
Taylor & Francis Verlag GmbH, Kaufingerstraße 24, 80331 München, Germany

www.ingramcontent.com/pod-product-compliance
Ingram Content Group UK Ltd.
Pitfield, Milton Keynes, MK11 3LW, UK
UKHW020956180425
457613UK00019B/713